Human Body Decom

Human Body Decomposition

Jarvis Hayman and Marc Oxenham

The School of Archaeology & Anthropology,
Australian National University,
Canberra, Australia

AMSTERDAM • BOSTON • HEIDELBERG • LONDON
NEW YORK • OXFORD • PARIS • SAN DIEGO
SAN FRANCISCO • SINGAPORE • SYDNEY • TOKYO

Academic Press is an imprint of Elsevier

Academic Press is an imprint of Elsevier
125 London Wall, London EC2Y 5AS, UK
525 B Street, Suite 1800, San Diego, CA 92101-4495, USA
50 Hampshire Street, 5th Floor, Cambridge, MA 02139, USA
The Boulevard, Langford Lane, Kidlington, Oxford OX5 1GB, UK

Notices
Knowledge and best practice in this field are constantly changing. As new research and
experience broaden our understanding, changes in research methods or professional practices,
may become necessary.

Practitioners and researchers must always rely on their own experience and knowledge in
evaluating and using any information or methods described herein. In using such information or
methods they should be mindful of their own safety and the safety of others, including parties for
whom they have a professional responsibility.

To the fullest extent of the law, neither the Publisher nor the authors, contributors, or editors,
assume any liability for any injury and/or damage to persons or property as a matter of products
liability, negligence or otherwise, or from any use or operation of any methods, products,
instructions, or ideas contained in the material herein.

Library of Congress Cataloging-in-Publication Data
A catalog record for this book is available from the Library of Congress

British Library Cataloguing-in-Publication Data
A catalogue record for this book is available from the British Library

ISBN: 978-0-12-803691-4

For Information on all Academic Press publications
visit our website at https://www.elsevier.com/

CONTENTS

BIOGRAPHY

Jarvis Hayman, FRCS (Ed), FRACS, MA (Hons), PhD

Jarvis Hayman graduated in Medicine at Aberdeen University. After moving to Australia in 1974, he worked for many years as a surgeon in Sydney and in a regional city in New South Wales. Upon retiring, he studied archeology at the Australian National University, obtaining a Master's degree in 2006 with a thesis on the archeology of the Scottish Highland Clearances. He then combined his archeological and medical knowledge to undertake a PhD in forensic archeology. Research for the thesis included a detailed study of the National Coronial Information System, based at the Victorian Institute of Forensic Medicine (VIFM) in Melbourne, studies of the autopsies of decomposed bodies at the VIFM and researching the decomposition of human bodies at the Grady Early Anthropology Research Facility (GEFARL) of the Texas State University in San Marcos. The thesis developed mathematical models using numerical total body scores of the decomposition process, to estimate the time of death up to 14 days, of human bodies found in many of the states of Australia.

Marc Oxenham, PhD, FSA

Marc Oxenham is a Reader in Archaeology and Biological Anthropology and an Australian Future Fellow at The Australian National University. He has played a leading role in understanding human biological (health and disease related) and cultural responses to significant human- and climate-induced events in Southeast Asia during the last 10,000 years. In addition to his close involvement over many years as an osteologist and archeologist with the Australian Defence Force's Unrecovered War Casualty-Army unit, he edited the first Australian focused book on forensic anthropology and allied disciplines in 2008 "Forensic Approaches to Death, Disaster and Abuse."

Over the last decade or so he has authored and edited 7 books and some 75 research papers and book chapters on topics ranging from forensic anthropology, paleopathology, bioarchaeology, paleoparasitology, to the archeology of children and the elderly.

From time immemorial when a decomposed or decomposing human body is discovered, those people with a questioning or scientific nature have asked three questions; how did this death happen, who was involved in the death, and what was the time of death. The answer to the third question will very often give clues which lead to answers to the first two questions.

The first known substantive written documentation of forensic methods and estimation of the time of death can be traced back to a 13th-century Sung dynasty medicolegal textbook entitled *Hsi Yuan Lu* (The Washing Away of Wrongs) by Sung Tz'u, a very astute legal official and death investigator in Fujian province, southern China. The modern era of scientific forensic investigation and the investigation into the time of death began at the beginning of the 19th century with Dr John Davy in Ceylon (Sri Lanka). Sporadic studies were published during the 19th century after which there was a notable paucity of studies, probably caused by two World Wars, until increasing numbers of studies began to be published from the 1950s until the present time.

During the time one of us (JH) was carrying out background research for a PhD thesis on the time since death in human bodies found decomposed in Australian conditions, it became apparent that a chronology of such research was lacking. There are numerous studies which begin with a short overview of the research but none which give a detailed account of it. On the basis that researchers need to know where they have come from to know where they are going to and that every researcher, figuratively speaking, stands on the shoulders of others, this work is presented. It has five chapters.

1. "Supravital Reactions in the Estimation of the Time Since Death (TSD)" deals with research in the stage immediately after death when the body undergoes changes but remains responsive to various stimuli.

2. "Algor Mortis and Temperature-Based Methods of Estimating the Time Since Death" deals with research during the phase when the body is cooling from normal body to ambient temperature.
3. "Biochemical Methods of Estimating the Time Since Death" covers research into methods using the changing biochemical reactions which occur and the chemical substances produced as the body decomposes.
4. "Research in the Later Stages of Decomposition" deals with the stage of decomposition after the onset of putrefaction and until skeletonisation occurs.
5. "Recent Research and Current Trends" in research into the TSD are outlined in the final chapter.

Throughout the book the terms TSD (time since death) and PMI (postmortem interval) are interchangeable.

CHAPTER 1

Supravital Reactions in the Estimation of the Time Since Death (TSD)

RIGOR MORTIS
LIVOR MORTIS
MEASUREMENT OF MECHANICAL AND ELECTRICAL EXCITABILITY OF MUSCLE
REFERENCES

Following the cessation of the heart and circulatory system at the moment of death, there is a period of time, generally accepted to be 3−4 minutes after the heart stops beating, during which some tissues remain responsive to various stimuli, and when resuscitation may be possible despite increasing anoxia of the tissues and resultant irreversible ischemia. However, it is not equivalent to the supravital period which is believed to extend from 100 to 120 minutes after cessation of the circulation (Madea, 2002a). During the supravital period, the tissues remain responsive to various electrical and mechanical stimuli and exhibit certain phenomena such as rigor mortis and livor mortis. Attempts have been made to use these reactions and phenomena to measure the time since death (TSD).

RIGOR MORTIS

The phenomenon of rigor mortis was first described in 1811 by the French physician, P.H. Nysten, but its physiological basis was not discovered until 1945 by Szent-Györgyi (2004). It consists of a sustained contraction of the muscles of the body, which begins at 2−6 hours after death, persists for 24−84 hours, and is then followed by gradual

Human Body Decomposition. DOI: http://dx.doi.org/10.1016/B978-0-12-803691-4.00001-7

relaxation until the muscles again become flaccid (Gill-King, 1997). The contractile units of muscle cells, sarcomeres, consist of parallel units of two types of protein, actin and myosin. Crosslinkages on the myosin units pull the actin units toward each other, causing muscle contraction. The process requires calcium and energy, the latter provided by adenosine triphosphate (ATP) (Bate-Smith and Bendall, 1947). The initial flaccidity of muscles after death is due to continued formation of ATP by anaerobic glycolysis, but with the passage of time, ATP is no longer resynthesized, energy is no longer available for the actin and myosin fibrils to remain relaxed and the fibrils contract, resulting in the muscle body as a whole contracting. Resolution of rigor mortis after 24–84 hours is caused by proteolytic enzymes within the muscle cells disrupting the myosin/actin units, causing the crosslinkages to break down and the muscles to relax (Gill-King, 1997).

At the beginning of the 19th century Nysten (1811), in France, carried out experiments on criminals immediately after their decapitation on the guillotine and he observed that rigor mortis began in the muscles of the jaw and then progressed distally to the feet and toes. This sequence was disputed by Shapiro (1950, 1954), who suggested that it began at the same time in all muscles but the variation in the sizes of the different joints and muscles meant that the larger muscles took longer to develop rigor mortis, giving the impression that it progressed from proximal to distal in the body. Krompecher designed an experiment to measure the intensity of rigor mortis in rat front limbs compared with rat hind limbs using different forces at different times during the course of rigor mortis (Krompecher and Fryc, 1978a). The hind limbs had a muscle mass 2.89 times the muscle mass of the front limbs. The results showed that although there was no difference between front and hind limbs with respect to the time taken to reach complete evolution of the rigor mortis, the onset and the relaxation of rigor mortis were more rapid in the front limbs which had the smaller muscle mass. In contrast, Kobayashi and colleagues (2001), experimenting with in vitro rat erector spinae muscles, found that although the volume of muscle samples varied there was no difference in the development and resolution of rigor mortis. They concluded that it was the proportion of muscle fiber types in each muscle, difference in temperature, and the dynamic characteristics of each joint that determined the speed of onset and resolution of rigor mortis.

Several intrinsic and extrinsic factors affect the speed of onset and duration of rigor mortis. Intrinsic factors such as violent exercise and high fever during the agonal stage will cause a rapid onset and shorter duration. The amount of skeletal muscle dictates the duration of rigor, for example, it appears and resolves early in infants but, in contrast, a robust physical person will have slower onset and a prolonged duration (Gill-King, 1997). This finding, however, was contradicted by Kobayashi and colleagues (2001). Krompecher and Fryc (1978b), in a study using rats, found that physical exercise before death caused an increased intensity of the rigor which reached its maximum intensity at the same time as normal controls but the maximum intensity was sustained longer. The rigor, however, reached resolution at the same time as the controls. In a controlled experiment using rats, Krompecher (1981) found that the higher the temperature, the shorter was the onset of rigor and the faster the resolution, a finding later confirmed by Kobayashi and colleagues (2001). At very low temperature (6°C), development was very slow at 48–60 hours and resolution very prolonged to 168 hours. This contrasted with a temperature of 37°C when development occurred at 3 hours and resolved at 6 hours. In a mortuary where corpses were kept refrigerated at 4°C, rigor was found to completely persist for 10 days in all corpses, became partial by 17 days, and resolved after 28 days (Varetto and Curto, 2005).

Other extrinsic factors which affect the course of rigor mortis are electrocution causing death, which accelerates the onset of rigor and shortens the duration, possibly because the violent cramps experienced cause a rapid fall in ATP (Krompecher and Bergerioux, 1988). Strychnine poisoning hastens the onset and duration of rigor mortis while carbon monoxide poisoning delays the resolution (Krompecher et al., 1983). If the rigidity of rigor mortis is broken by force it can re-establish itself if the process is still ongoing; the re-establishment begins immediately after being broken, the rigidity is weaker but the maximum extent of it is the same as in controls, as is the course of resolution (Krompecher et al., 2008).

Objective measurement of the force required to break the rigidity of rigor mortis was attempted for many years, the first attempt being made in 1919 by Oppenheim and Wacker, but the difficulty in measuring this force is that the strength of the force varies with the stage of development and resolution of the rigor mortis (Krompecher, 2002). The forces involved are initially small, rising rapidly to a maximum, and then reducing gradually over time until resolution occurs. One measurement at one period of time in the duration of the rigor will not reveal any useful information concerning the estimation of the TSD. Krompecher (1994) carried out experiments on groups of rats killed by a standard method and kept at the same temperature of 24°C post mortem. The same force, insufficient to break the rigor, was applied to a limb at varying intervals after death up to 48 hours. It was found that repeated measurements of the intensity of rigor mortis allowed a more accurate estimation of the TSD than a single measurement and Krompecher suggested certain guidelines: (1) If there was an increase in intensity, the initial measurements were taken no earlier than 5 hours post mortem. (2) If there was a decrease in intensity the initial measurements were taken no earlier than 7 hours post mortem. (3) At 24 hours postmortem resolution was complete and no further change in intensity should occur. A recent study of 79 deceased patients was undertaken in a hospital mortuary where the time of death was known, where they were all transported to the mortuary within 5 hours and kept at a temperature of 20−21°C (Anders et al., 2013). The aims of the study were to determine if re-establishment of rigor mortis took place in loosened joints after more than 8 hours and, if so, could it be determined how many hours postmortem re-establishment of rigor mortis did occur? Deaths occurred from a variety of disease conditions but because of the small numbers, no correction was possible for disease state. Rigor mortis was loosened in 174 joints of 44 deceased persons between 7.5 and 10.5 hours post mortem to determine whether re-establishment occurred after 8 hours and 140 joints were examined after loosening at 15−21 hours post mortem to determine how many hours postmortem re-establishment could occur. The study found that 121 of 314 joints (38.5%) showed re-establishment of rigor mortis between 7.5 and 19 hours and the authors concluded that the currently accepted view that rigor mortis could only be studied to determine the time of death less than 8 hours post mortem, required re-evaluation by further studies. Attempts have been made to standardize the measurement of the force of rigidity in rigor mortis but they have not received widespread acceptance (Schuck et al., 1979; Vain et al., 1992). Because of the subjective nature of the assessment of rigor mortis and the number of variable factors determining its onset, duration, and resolution, it should only be used in conjunction with other methods when estimating TSD (Henssge and Madea, 2002).

LIVOR MORTIS

Livor mortis or lividity is the gravitational pooling of blood in the dependent parts of the body, both externally in the skin capillaries and venules but also in the internal organs. Its onset is variable but it is usually most evident about 2 hours after death, although it is stated to occur as soon as 15 minutes after death (Clark et al., 1997). Initially the color is red but it later becomes purple as oxygen dissociates from the hemoglobin, changing it to purple-colored deoxyhemoglobin. This color change can be variable depending on the circumstances of death and the environment. Cold temperatures will delay the dissociation of oxygen from the hemoglobin, delaying the color change from red to purple. Carbon monoxide poisoning produces a persistent cherry red color and cyanide poisoning will also cause the red color to persist. Lividity may not be seen in bodies that are very anemic at death. Initially it is not fixed, that is, if pressure is applied to a skin area the red color changes to white as the blood is returned to the capillaries due to the pressure. Bodies lying on a hard surface will also show white blanching in the areas making contact with the surface for the same reason. Lividity is said to become fixed in 4–6 hours, that is, the red color no longer disappears on pressure because with cooling of the body, the fat surrounding the capillaries solidifies, constricting the capillaries and preventing the return of blood into them (Clark et al., 1997).

A reference to lividity occurs in the earliest extant comprehensive handbook for mid-13th-century Chinese forensic investigators into homicides and other deaths by Sung Tz'u. A clear description of lividity occurs toward the end of Sung Tz'u's (1186–1249) handbook: "Generally, dead persons have a slight red coloration on the back of the neck, on the top of the back, on the ribs, the back of the waist, the insides of the legs, the knees, the feet and the stomach. Check to determine if after death these corpses were laid out supine overnight. The collapse of the blood vessels may cause this slight red coloration, which does not indicate any other cause of death."

Turning to more recent times, the time sequence of livor mortis has been proposed as a method of estimating the TSD. However, the physiological mechanism of blood pooling, coagulation, and hemoglobin dissociation is so variable as to make it an unreliable method (Knight, 2002). The assessment by observation with the passage of time is subjective and therefore prone to observer error. Recently attempts have been made to quantify the hypostasis of lividity by colorimetry. A preliminary study carried out by Vanezis (1991), using a colorimeter, showed a linear relationship between the passage of time and the lightening color intensity when bodies showing lividity in dependent areas were turned over to enable blood to return to capillaries. Hypostasis reduced considerably even after 24 hours and slightly up to 3 days after death. In a follow-up study, Vanezis and Trujillo (1996) attempted to quantify the rate of change in the intensity of livor mortis with time by the use of a colorimeter. Ninety-three cadavers in whom the time of death was known to within 3 hours were subjected to colorimetric study. The bodies, kept at 4°C, were placed in the prone position and the degree of luminosity on their backs measured at 4-hourly intervals up to 72 hours. A strong correlation was found between the degree of luminosity and the postmortem interval (PMI), lividity becoming darker with increasing PMI in an exponential fashion. After 72 hours lividity became fixed. There were only a small number of cases in this series and the authors concluded that factors such as body size, cause of death, body position, environmental temperature, and especially skin color could affect the luminosity.

A simple colorimeter was developed by Masashi Inoue and colleagues (1994) to measure the change in intensity of postmortem lividity with the passage of time. The colorimeter transmitted and received light in the 600-nm wavelength region which was poorly absorbed by the water and melanin of the skin but was strongly absorbed by hemoglobin. The instrument was used to measure the intensity of lividity as pressure was applied to areas of maximum and minimum lividity in 42 corpses whose PMI was known, over a period of time until lividity became fixed. A strong correlation between the passage of time and the intensity of the livor mortis was found but there were variations caused by the same factors that others had noted, namely, body size, cause of death, posture, environmental temperature, and skin color. Kaatsch and colleagues (1994) measured pressure-induced blanching of livor mortis to estimate TSD with a digital system of photometric quantification on 50 cadavers in which the time of death was known. The authors used defined magnitudes of pressure, in contrast to subjective pressure by finger or forceps. They found distinct differences between the different time categories for pressure-induced color changes in lividity up to 40 hours post mortem, after which pressure no longer produced blanching. They also found that blanching could be produced for a longer period of time in bodies stored at a cooler temperature. There were wide variations in the data which they attributed to skin color, antemortem physical condition, cause of death, environmental factors such as ambient temperature, and storage conditions prior to measurement. The authors concluded that provided these factors were taken into account, and considering this was a small study, the findings provided a basis for further research to improve the measurement of lividity.

The quantitative measurements of livor mortis are only useful for 30–40 hours post mortem and before the changes of putrefaction have begun (Kaatsch et al., 1994). The rate of occurrence, intensity of coloration, distribution, and possible redistribution of lividity are so variable and difficult to standardize that they should not be used alone to estimate the postmortem period (Vanezis and Trujillo, 1996).

MEASUREMENT OF MECHANICAL AND ELECTRICAL EXCITABILITY OF MUSCLE

The first recorded observation of the effect of mechanical muscle stimulation in an isolated postmortem limb was by Dowler (1846), when he struck the biceps muscle in an extended arm with the edge of his hand, 2 hours after death, causing the arm to contract so that the hand struck the breast. Most research into the use of the response of muscles to mechanical stimulation in the postmortem period has been carried out by researchers in Germany and published in the German language (Madea, 2002b; Henssge et al., 1988). Skeletal muscle is responsive to mechanical stimulation in the immediate postmortem period and the muscular contraction can be measured. When the lower third of the thigh above the patella is struck, there is a strong muscle contraction response for 1.5–2.5 hours, gradually becoming weaker until there is no response after about 12 hours (Madea, 2002b). The upper time limit of idiomuscular response was based on a few case studies in the earlier part of the 20th century but an upper time limit of 13 hours when no further response occurs has been recently confirmed by a large study on 270 cases, the majority of which were of sudden death and in all of which the time of death was known precisely (Warther et al., 2012). The practical use of this method is limited and it should not be used as the sole method of estimation of the TSD (Madea, 2002b).

In 1781, Luigi Galvani carried out a series of experiments on dissected frogs in which the thighs were entirely removed from the body, leaving the legs and feet attached to a stump of the vertebral column by the sciatic nerves alone (Hoff, 1936). In experiments using a machine which produced electricity, as well as using atmospheric electricity, he stimulated the sciatic nerves and the vertebral columns, which caused the muscles of the frogs' legs to contract. He attributed this to "animal electricity" which was distributed along the nerves to the muscles of the legs. Further studies were carried out in the 19th century and toward the end of that century and in the first half of the 20th century studies were directed toward the use of electrical excitability as a means of determining the TSD, specifically as indicated by the lack of electrical excitability of muscle (Madea, 2002c). From the 1960s to the 1990s most studies were carried out in Germany and reported in the German language (Madea, 2002c). Most of the research in this period was confined to giving a description and subjective grading of the muscular response to electrical stimulation according to the strength of contraction and spread of movement to areas distant from the stimulus. The results of various studies were not comparable because the position of the electrodes, the parameters of excitation, and the grade of muscular contraction were not standardized (Madea and Henssge, 1990). Madea and Henssge (1990) reviewed the use of electrical stimulation of muscle tissue and its efficacy in estimating the TSD and, for the first time, measured and quantified the force of contraction in the orbicularis oculi muscle as it declined with the passage of time. They stated that it was important that the method be standardized and they formulated a protocol for its use at the scene of a death with which the time of death, especially in the period 3–8 hours after death, could be determined. By combining this method of stimulation of the orbicularis oculi muscle with the use of the nomogram method of determining the TSD by temperature measurement (Henssge, 1988) as well as the assessment of lividity, rigor mortis, and the mechanical stimulation of muscle, the accuracy of estimating the TSD was increased (Henssge et al., 1988). A study by Madea (1992) determined that the length of time after death that the muscle remained responsive to electrical stimulation, could be up to 13 hours. There was a period of maximum contraction and a period of relaxation until the muscle response was exhausted. The decrease of the maximum force by which the muscle could be stimulated to contract and the increase in the relaxation time could both be measured. The period of responsiveness showed interindividual variation depending on the amount of glycogen in the muscles at the time of death, which in turn determined the period of elasticity of the muscles before the onset of rigor mortis. Further studies were required using simultaneous measurement of electrical excitability of the muscle and parameters of anaerobic glycolysis, probably lactate concentration, in order to increase the accuracy of measurement of the TSD. A second factor determining the period of muscle responsiveness was the environmental temperature; the lower the temperature the longer was the response.

Other research using electrical stimulation to improve estimation of the TSD in the very early postmortem period has been carried out by McDowall and colleagues (1998) who measured the absolute refractory period (ARP) in the sciatic nerves of newly killed rats. The ARP is the interval immediately following an action potential when a nerve is unable to propagate a further action potential in response to stimulation. McDowall and colleagues found that measuring the ARP did not provide a more accurate estimation of the PMI than the use of rectal temperature but when both variables were used in combination, the overall accuracy was improved. Skeletal muscle only remains indirectly excitable to stimulation for about 1.5 hours after death and therefore this short time period during which the ARP could be measured meant that the practical usefulness of this technique was limited to a small number of cases in which it was necessary to determine whether or not death was instantaneous. Similar research was carried out by Elmas and colleagues (2001) and Querido and Phillips used extracellular abdominal impedance of an electrical current as a means of estimating the PMI. None of these recent methods have improved the estimation of the TSD in the early postmortem period (Querido, 1994, 2000; Querido and Phillips, 2001).

In conclusion, the use of any one supravital reaction to estimate the PMI in the early period after death, up to about 13 hours, is not to be recommended. Instead a combination of methods as suggested by Henssge and colleagues (1988) remains the best approach at the present time.

REFERENCES

Anders, S., Kunz, M., Gehl, A., Sehner, S., Raupach, T., Beck-Bornholdt, H.-P., 2013. Estimation of the time since death- reconsidering the re-establishment of rigor mortis. Int. J. Legal Med. 127, 127–130.

Bate-Smith, E.C., Bendall, J.R., 1947. Rigor mortis and adenosine triphosphate. J. Physiol. 106, 177–185.

Clark, M.A., Worrell, M.B., Pless, J.E., 1997. Post-mortem changes in soft tissues. In: Haglund, W.D., Sorg, M.H. (Eds.), Forensic Taphonomy: The Post-mortem Fate of Human Remains. CRC Press, Boca Raton, pp. 151–164.

Dowler, B., 1846. Experimental researches on the post-mortem contractility of the muscles, with observations on the reflex theory. N.Y. J. Med. 8, 305–339.

Elmas, I., Baslo, B., Ertas, M., Kaya, M., 2001. Analysis of gastrocnemius compound muscle action potential in rat after death: significance for the estimation of early post-mortem interval. Forensic Sci. Int. 116, 125–132.

Gill-King, H., 1997. Chemical and ultrastructural aspects of decomposition. In: Haglund, W.D., Sorg, M.H. (Eds.), Forensic Taphonomy: The Post-mortem Fate of Human Remains. CRC Press, Boca Raton, pp. 93–108.

Henssge, C., 1988. Death time estimation in case work part I: the rectal temperature time of death nomogram. Forensic Sci. Int. 38, 209–236.

Henssge, C., Madea, B., 2002. Practical casework. In: Knight, B. (Ed.), Estimation of the Time since Death in the Early Post-mortem Period, second ed. Edward Arnold, pp. 244–261.

Henssge, C., Madea, B., Gallenkemper, E., 1988. Death time estimation in casework II: integration of different methods. Forensic Sci. Int. 39, 77–87.

Hoff, H.E., 1936. Galvani and the pre-Galvanian electrophysiologists. Ann. Sci. 1 (2), 157–172.

Inoue, M., et al., 1994. Development of an instrument to measure post-mortem lividity and its preliminary application to estimate the time since death. Forensic Sci. Int. 65, 185–193.

Kaatsch, H.-J., Schmidtke, E., Nietsch, W., 1994. Photometric measurement of pressure induced blanching of livor mortis as an aid to estimating the time of death. Int. J. Legal Med. 106, 209–214.

Knight, B., 2002. Hypostasis and timing of death. In: Knight, B. (Ed.), Estimation of the Time since Death in the Early Post-mortem Period, second ed. Edward Arnold, pp. 206–208.

Kobayashi, M., Ikegaya, H., Takase, I., Hatanaka, K., Sakurada, K., Iwase, H., 2001. Development of rigor mortis is not affected by muscle volume. Forensic Sci. Int. 117, 213–219.

Krompecher, T., 2002. Rigor mortis: estimation of the time since death by evaluation of cadaveric rigidity. In: Knight, B. (Ed.), Estimation of the Time since Death in the Early Post-mortem Period, second ed. Edward Arnold, pp. 144–160.

Krompecher, T., 1981. Experimental evaluation of rigor mortis: V. Effect of various temperatures on the evolution of rigor mortis. Forensic Sci. Int. 17, 19–26.

Krompecher, T., 1994. Experimental evaluation of rigor mortis: VIII. Estimation of time since death by repeated measurements of intensity of rigor mortis on rats. Forensic Sci. Int. 68, 149–159.

Krompecher, T., Bergerioux, C., 1988. Experimental evaluation of rigor mortis: VII. Effect of ante- and post-mortem electrocution on the evolution of rigor mortis. Forensic Sci. Int. 38, 27–35.

Krompecher, T., Fryc, O., 1978a. Experimental evaluation of rigor mortis: III. Comparative study of the evolution of rigor mortis in different sized muscle groups in rats. Forensic Sci. Int. 12, 97–102.

Krompecher, T., Fryc, O., 1978b. Experimental evaluation of rigor mortis: IV. Change in strength and evolution of rigor mortis in the case of physical exercise preceding death. Forensic Sci. Int. 12, 103–107.

Krompecher, T., Bergerioux, C., Brandt-Casadevall, C., Gujer, H.-R., 1983. Experimental evaluation of rigor mortis: VI. Effect of various causes of death on the evolution of rigor mortis. Forensic Sci. Int. 22, 1–9.

Krompecher, T., Gilles, A., Brandt-Casadevall, C., Mangin, P., 2008. Experimental evaluation of rigor mortis: IX. The influence of the breaking (mechanical solution) on the development of rigor mortis. Forensic Sci. Int. 176, 157–162.

Madea, B., 1992. Estimating the time of death from measurement of the electrical excitability of skeletal muscle. Forensic Sci. Soc. J. 32 (2), 117–129.

Madea, B., 2002a. Supravitality in tissues. In: Knight, B. (Ed.), Estimation of the Time Since Death in the Early Post-mortem Period, second ed. Edward Arnold, pp. 135–142.

Madea, B., 2002b. Post-mortem mechanical excitation of skeletal muscle. In: Knight, B. (Ed.), Estimation of the Time Since Death in the Early Post-mortem Period, second ed. Edward Arnold, pp. 160–164.

Madea, B., 2002c. Post mortem electrical excitability of skeletal muscle in case work. In: Knight, B. (Ed.), Estimation of the Time Since Death in the Early Post-mortem Period, second ed. Edward Arnold, pp. 164–206.

Madea, B., Henssge, C., 1990. Electrical excitability of skeletal muscle post-mortem in casework. Forensic Sci. Int. 47, 207–227.

McDowall, K.L., Lenihan, D.V., Busuttil, A., Glasby, M.A., 1998. The use of absolute refractory period in the estimation of early post-mortem interval. Forensic Sci. Int. 91, 163–170.

Nysten, P.H., 1811. Quatrième Section, Article Premier; De la contractilité des organs musculaire au présumés tels chez l'hommes et les animaux sang rouges, après les divers genres de mort violente, Recherches de physiologie et de chimie pathologiques pour faire suite a celles de Bichat sur la vie et la mort. Paris, 1811.

Querido, D., 1994. Time-dependent changes in electrical resistance of the intact abdomen during the 1-504 hour post-mortem period in rats. Forensic Sci. Int. 67, 17–25.

Querido, D., 2000. Temperature correction of abdominal impedance: improved relationship between impedance and post-mortem interval. Forensic Sci. Int. 109, 39–50.

Querido, D., Phillips, M.R.B., 2001. Estimation of post-mortem interval, temperature correction of extracellular abdominal impedance during the first 21 days of death. Forensic Sci. Int. 116, 133–138.

Schuck, M., Beier, G., Liebhardt, E., Spann, W., 1979. On the estimation of lay time by measurements of rigor mortis. Forensic Sci. Int. 14, 171–176.

Shapiro, H.A., 1950. Rigor mortis. Br. Med. J. 2 (4673), 304.

Shapiro, H.A., 1954. Medico-legal mythology. J. Forensic Med. 1, 144–169.

Sung Tz'u, 1186–1249. The Washing Away of Wrongs. Translated from the Chinese by McKnight, B.E., 1981. University of Michigan, Ann Arbor, p. 152.

Szent-Györgyi, A.G., 2004. The early history of the biochemistry of muscle contraction. J. Gen. Physiol. 123, 631–641.

Vain, A., Kaupilla, R., Humal, L.-H., Vuori, E., 1992. Grading rigor mortis with myotonometry – a new possibility to estimate time of death. Forensic Sci. Int. 56, 147–150.

Vanezis, P., 1991. Assessing hypostasis by colorimetry. Forensic Sci. Int. 52, 1–3.

Vanezis, P., Trujillo, O., 1996. Evaluation of hypostasis using a colorimeter measuring system and its application to assessment of the post-mortem interval (time of death). Forensic Sci. Int. 78, 19–28.

Varetto, L., Curto, O., 2005. Long persistence of rigor mortis at constant low temperature. Forensic Sci. Int. 147, 31–34.

Warther, S., et al., 2012. Estimation of the time since death: post-mortem contractions of skeletal muscles following mechanical stimulation (idiomuscular contraction). Int. J. Legal Med. 126, 399–405.

CHAPTER 2

Algor Mortis and Temperature-Based Methods of Estimating the Time Since Death

Algor mortis refers to the cooling of the body after death until it reaches ambient temperature. Methods of estimating the postmortem interval (PMI) from the rate of fall in temperature have been studied more extensively than any other stage in the decomposition process. During life, the normal body temperature of 37.4°C is maintained. After death the rate of heat loss depends on several factors which include the ambient temperature conditions, body mass, whether or not there was fever immediately prior to death, the presence or absence of clothing, and the body position. A time lag of variable interval occurs before the body begins to cool, as a result of a temperature gradient developing between the core and the surface of the body.

Human Body Decomposition. DOI: http://dx.doi.org/10.1016/B978-0-12-803691-4.00002-9

EARLY RESEARCH IN THE 19TH CENTURY

Although the development of the thermometer has been attributed to several inventors over the centuries, it was Sir Thomas Clifford Allbutt who developed the clinical thermometer in 1870, replacing the foot-long instrument that took 20 minutes to register a patient's temperature (Underwood, 1951). This invention provided an impetus to research, including the estimation of time since death (TSD) in the early postmortem period.

The first researcher in the modern era to suggest that the loss of temperature after death might be useful as a basis for the estimation of the PMI was Dr John Davy (1839), who conducted studies on the bodies of 10 British soldiers who had died in Malta in 1828. Autopsies and observations were made at times which varied from 2 to 17.5 hours after death. Observing that the temperature of the internal organs seemed to be higher than the external surface of the bodies and the environmental temperatures, Davy took temperature measurements from under the left ventricles of the heart and from under the liver and he also recorded the room temperatures. All bodies apart from two had died from or with infection and as a result would have had a raised temperature before death. In all cases he found the temperature of the internal body to be raised above room temperature. He repeated his observations on nine soldiers who had died in a hospital in Chatham, Kent, in 1838 with similar findings. Autopsy times after death varied from 4.5 to 29 hours, and all cases except for one had some form of infection at the time of death. He attributed the higher internal temperatures to an unknown "heat-generating process," as well as to the febrile disease. This study used a limited number of cases, employed crude methods of observation and the time intervals after death when the observations were made varied, but the conclusion that these observations "may enable the enquirer......to arrive at a tolerably positive conclusion, in doubtful cases of death, as to the time which may have elapsed, between the fatal event and the post mortem examination" (Davy, 1839, pp. 247−248) pointed the way toward further research in this field.

Taylor and Wilks (1863) published a study of a series of 100 bodies admitted to a morgue. They recorded the age, time of death, cause of death, humidity of the air, and postmortem temperature of each body, two to four observations being carried out on each body at varying intervals up to 17 hours after being admitted to the morgue. However, the time of taking the first readings varied from the time of death up to 12 hours after death. The temperatures were taken by placing the thermometer bulb on the abdominal skin and the recordings could therefore have varied with the ambient temperature change. The temperature of the morgue was also recorded but in some of the cases there was no record of the length of time before temperature measurements were commenced. Although the conditions of the study were not controlled, Taylor and Wilks made several pertinent observations that laid the basis for future research. Firstly, the temperature of "fat" bodies remained at a higher temperature for a longer period than thin or emaciated bodies and that moisture in the atmosphere appeared to favor decomposition much more than heat. Secondly, bodies cooled slowly and progressively, retaining considerable heat for upwards of 12 hours after death and the temperature of the internal body organs remained at a higher temperature than the skin for a longer period. Thirdly, they recognized that the environment in which a body was found, and coverings, or lack of, on a body could modify the rate at which a body cooled. Lastly, they observed that in certain circumstances such as a person dying of fever or found with heavy body coverings, an initial rise in temperature occurred before a steady fall but they did not observe the temperature plateau before the fall in temperature. Taylor and Wilks (1863, p. 202) concluded that "the changes which take place in a dead body before the commencement of putrefaction, may, if accurately observed, enable a medical witness to form an opinion of the time at which the deceased died."

Rainy (1868) produced a prescient study in which he recognized that the evidence of TSD depended not only on the excess of body temperature over that of the surrounding medium but also on the presence and duration of rigor mortis and the presence and progress of chemical decomposition. He was the first to recognize that the cooling of a cadaver does not follow Newton's law of cooling (Winterton, 1999). Rainy detailed a study of postmortem temperature measurements on 46 bodies up to 63 hours after death. He recognized the necessity of standardizing the study conditions by attempting to take the measurements in a room with still air at a uniform temperature. Therefore the observations on 54 bodies out of 100 at the beginning of the study were discarded because the temperature of the morgue did not remain steady, which was necessary in order to eliminate as far as possible all circumstances which might complicate the law of cooling. He also would have wished the observations to have been made at the same intervals after death but admitted that this was impracticable because of the varying times over a 24-hour period at which the cases had died. Measurements were taken from the abdominal skin at the umbilicus and from the rectum. The temperature of the morgue and three rectal temperature readings were recorded in all cases and four readings in 18 cases. Rainy then calculated the "ratio per hour" at which the temperature was found to vary by determining how much the temperature of the rectum varied above ambient temperature at the start of the measuring process and for each hour thereafter. Rainy observed that bodies placed in a colder medium gradually lost heat until they reached the temperature of the medium but the rate of cooling slowed as the temperature of the body approached that of the medium. He recognized that this pattern of cooling of a cadaver did not follow Newton's empirical law of cooling which states that the rate of loss of temperature of a hot body is directly proportional to the difference of temperature between its surface and the surrounding cool medium (Winterton, 1999). When the difference between the surrounding environment and the body temperature was "moderate," by which he presumably meant low, the rate of cooling very nearly approximated the law but when the difference was greater, body temperature was found to rise before gradually cooling at a steady rate and then at a slower rate as it approached ambient temperature. His description was essentially that of the temperature plateau before the fall in body temperature and then a slower fall to ambient temperature, the cooling curve first described in the 20th century by Shapiro (1954). He could not explain the initial temperature plateau and the later more rapid fall in temperature other than by "the gradual cessation of the calorific processes which, in the earlier stages, retard the cooling" (Rainy, 1868, p. 328). Rainy stressed the need for two rectal temperature measurements, taken at least an hour apart, emphasizing that a precise time of death could not be given, but only a maximum and a minimum period during which death could have occurred. He devised a formula which calculated the number of hours since death but the time calculated by his formula would, in almost every case, be less than the actual TSD because of the slower cooling of the body in the early stage. Rainy stated that it was more difficult to give a maximum number of hours, but that from observation of cases in which the temperature of the rectum was found to be below 85°F (29.4°C), the time elapsed since death was not less than the time deduced from the formula multiplied by 1.5. This figure of 1.5 was also quoted by Glaister (1942) when he suggested the use of the following formula as a method of estimating the time of death;

$$\text{Approx. hours since death} = \frac{(\text{Normal temp. } 98.4°F(36.9°C) - \text{Rectal temp.})}{1.5}$$

(2.1)

As late as 1973 this formula was quoted as being useful, when it was stated that a body tended to lose heat at the rate of 1.5°F (0.8°C) per hour (Rentoul and Smith, 1973). Even at the present time this figure is still used as an approximate rate of heat loss (Clark et al., 1997).

Burman (1880) recorded the temperature of nine cadavers from the moment of death for varying periods as they cooled. Recordings were taken with a long-handled thermometer bent at a right angle and placed in the axilla so that the temperature could be read without disturbing its placement in the axilla. Recordings were taken at least every hour and in some cases more frequently. Burman recognized the importance of measuring internal body temperature because the internal organs remained at a higher temperature than the exterior of the body and that there was a gradient of heat loss from the interior of the body to the external body surface but he regretted that he did not do this. He also acknowledged the effect of the various different environmental factors such as the environmental temperature, whether the body was in air or water, and the amount and nature of clothing in determining the rate of cooling, and he tried to standardize environmental conditions as much as possible. He calculated that the average rate of cooling was 1.6°F (0.8°C) per hour and he concluded that the estimated number of hours since death could be calculated by subtracting the axillary temperature from the temperature at the time of death, which he assumed was 98.4°F (36.9°C). Burman (1880) recognized that the temperature could, in some cases, rise above 98.4°F (36.9°C) after death but he dismissed this as being a rare occurrence. He noted an initial rapid fall in temperature in the first few hours after death and that the higher the original temperature at death, the faster was the initial fall in temperature but that the cooling of a body was slower than had been generally thought. Even after 30 hours a body may retain a temperature 2−3°F above that of the room.

Womack (1887) used a series of mathematical calculations to come to the conclusion that a cadaver did not cool as quickly as a liquid would by radiation and convection under similar conditions. Remarkably he claimed to be able to accurately determine cadaver temperature to within 0.025°F by using a very thin glass thermometer with a mercury bulb strapped to the abdominal wall. He acknowledged that cooling of the cadaver was affected by a number of variable factors which included the unknown temperature at death, the varying temperature of the atmosphere, coverings or lack of on the body, and the locality of the body. He did not recognize the initial temperature plateau or subsequent rapid fall before the slower decline in temperature as it reached ambient temperature. Womack attempted to achieve a great degree of accuracy with conditions which were not controlled or standardized.

From the latter part of the 19th century until the mid-20th century, no papers of practical value were published, possibly because of the intervention of the Boer War and two World Wars, and research into TSD did not advance. In this respect it is interesting to note that Burman (1880) recognized the inaccuracy of using the then customary method of gauging the temperature of the skin of a body by using the back of the hand. In all cases he advocated the use of a thermometer. However, even as late as 1921 research had advanced no further, as was illustrated by Dr E.M. Vaughan, a Medical Assistant District Attorney in Brooklyn, when he described an elaborate method of approximately estimating the time of death by touching various parts of the body extremities (Vaughan, 1921).

MID-20TH CENTURY RESEARCH

1950 to 1960: Early Attempts to Determine the TSD in the Early Postmortem Period

A summary of the state of research into the estimation of TSD in the early 1950s was given by F.J. Cairns in 1952 when he outlined the factors which modified body cooling immediately after death (Cairns and Forbes, 1952). These were the effect of different environmental temperatures, whether the body was clothed or naked and found in water or on dry land. Various authorities had quoted formulae and he recognized that an important modifying factor was the temperature at the time of death. The biochemical mechanism of rigor mortis still had not been elucidated and as a method of estimating the TSD it was falling into disfavor. In fact, the estimation of TSD at this time was still an observational and qualitative exercise based on experience and only an approximation could be given. In the same article, J.A. Forbes outlined a study of some cooling curves from cadavers at the Royal Melbourne Hospital (Cairns and Forbes, 1952). Temperatures had been recorded from the upper part of the abdomen, liver, thorax, rectum, thigh, and brain. Intraabdominal temperatures were obtained through a puncture wound below the right lobe of the liver and recordings from this position showed continued heat production after death with the curves showing a rise, then a plateau, before a fall. The environmental temperature and obesity affected the rate of fall but overall there was inconsistency in the estimation of the TSD. If a certain temperature was selected there was a great variation between cases in the number of hours since death, while if a certain TSD was selected the corresponding intra-abdominal temperatures were widely scattered in comparable cases so that the estimation of the TSD seemed impossible. On the other hand, Forbes found that the temperature curves from the brains were logarithmic in form and ran in a parallel fashion, thus conforming to Newton's law of cooling, suggesting that further work might provide data for a more accurate estimation of the TSD.

A study reported by Schwarz and Heidenwolf (1953) set the pattern of research that would occur during the rest of the century. Their opinion was that not enough emphasis had been given until that time, of determining the time of death from the temperature of the body. They studied 39 adult bodies, in 16 of which the time of death was known. Of the remaining 23 cases studied, only 9 had not died with a fever. They established cooling curves in 25 bodies which had not died with a fever and in which the temperature at the time of death was 37°C. The authors found that when the environmental conditions were standardized, cooling was exclusively due to the difference between the temperature of the interior of the body and that of the surrounding atmosphere. Cooling was more rapid initially because of the greater difference in temperature between the body and the surrounding air. In cases dying with a fever, they stated that no definite conclusions could be drawn as to the time of death from postmortem cooling as the temperature may continue to rise after death due to the presence and action of microorganisms and this would affect the rate of cooling to an unknown extent.

All cases had the temperature taken from a thermometer inserted in the anus and the cooling curves they established recognized the slow reduction of temperature at the start of cooling which they attributed to the slower cooling of the interior of the body until it reached equilibrium with the surface. In none of the cases was there an initial rise in temperature before a fall. The temperature then fell more rapidly but progressively and then more slowly as it approached equilibrium with the surrounding atmosphere, reaching ambient temperature after about 36 hours. The estimation of the TSD became less accurate as the speed of cooling decreased toward ambient temperature due to inevitable variations in room temperature. Apart from premortem fever, another intrinsic factor influencing the rate of cooling was the ratio between the surface area and the unit weight of the body. The study was on unclothed bodies but their judgment was that the influence of clothing seemed to cause the same variation as the difference in size of the body. Schwarz and Heidenwolf seem to have been the first to suggest the necessity of determining a mathematical formula, incorporating the various factors affecting a body cooling, in order to estimate the time of death but that an exact mathematical definition which would take into account various additional thermal influences would be too complex considering the great variability of the factors concerned in the loss of heat (Fig. 2.1).

The present, more scientific era of research into the estimation of TSD began when De Saram and colleagues (1955) recorded the temperature fall in a series of 41 bodies of executed prisoners in Ceylon (Sri Lanka). It was possible to control the conditions of the collection, storage, and recording of the bodies much more closely than in previous studies because the prisoners were all executed at 8 am in the morning. Recording of the body temperatures was standardized by taking rectal temperatures from 3 to 4 inches (7.6 to 10.2 cm) within the rectum. Readings were taken half-hourly for 12 hours. The bodies were all examined in the same room in Colombo except for five which were executed in Kandy but where conditions were different but similarly controlled. Room temperatures and humidity

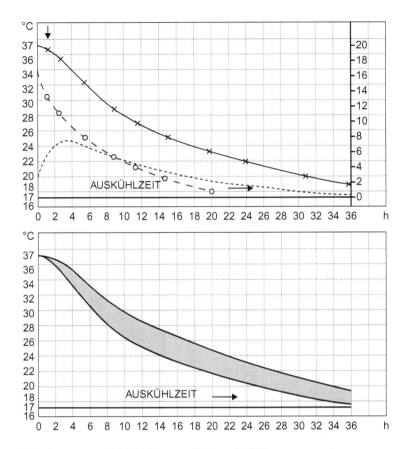

Figure 2.1 Cooling curves established by Schwarz and Heidenwolf (1953).

were recorded. The observations confirmed in all cases that there was a lag period in temperature of 45 minutes, when it remained essentially the same, before a rapid fall and then a slowing as temperature reached that of the room. The authors recognized that the difference between the body temperature and room temperature did have a significant effect on the cooling rate. Conduction, radiation, and especially evaporation which depended on the ambient humidity were also important factors. The body size factor which incorporated body weight and surface area was also important. Clothing on the bodies did not significantly influence the rate of heat loss. By a complex process, a formula was calculated which incorporated the influence of some of the modifying factors, except the body size factor and humidity and it was suggested that this could be used with reasonable accuracy within 8 hours of death, if the room temperature remained constant and an initial rectal temperature of 99.6°F (37.6°C) was assumed. These conditions, however, cannot be controlled in normal practice.

Shapiro (1954) drew attention to the initial temperature plateau after death, during which time the body temperature did not fall, essentially the same finding that Rainy (1868) had made. Shapiro found that this plateau could be maintained for up to 4 hours and he attributed this to the temperature gradient between the central body core and the external surface, the surface cooling occurring before the central organs.

Lyle and Cleveland studied (1956) 69 bodies over 2 years with the purpose of determining the rate of postmortem cooling in the first 24 hours. The times of death were known, the time before measurements began was as short as possible, and thermocouples were used to measure the temperature from the exposed skin of the forehead and the covered skin of the chest. Thermocouples recording rectal temperature were placed in water-tight gold-filled tubes and the liver, quadriceps muscle of the thigh, and brain thermocouples were attached to 19 gauge needles. Environmental conditions were as standardized as possible: 24 cases were in a room kept between 75°F and 78°F (23.9°C and 25.6°C), 22 cases between 65°F and 68°F (18.3°C and 20°C), and 23 cases between 62°F and 78°F (16.7°C and 25.6°C). Time−temperature charts were constructed for each case incorporating the fall in temperature from each site. Lyle and Cleveland (1956) showed that the rate of heat loss varied considerably depending on the site of recording. The range of temperature variability was less in the brain and progressively more variable in the rectum, liver, muscle, and skin. They concluded that the rate of heat loss depended on the environmental temperature as well as body structure, physiological activity, putrefaction, and external insulation and that the time of death by measurement of heat loss was not satisfactory after 24 hours post mortem. These factors had less effect on heat loss from the brain than from the other organs. In contrast to Shapiro's previous study 2 years earlier (Shapiro, 1954), Lyle and Cleveland (1956) did not recognize any temperature plateau before the more rapid fall in temperature. The authors admitted they were not primarily concerned with establishing the TSD but rather with establishing rates of heat loss under known conditions. This was because they believed that determining the exact time of death could be accomplished only after the establishment of rates of heat loss from the body when conditions were controlled as well as when conditions were variable.

A study of over 100 bodies during a 4-year period admitted to a morgue was made by Fiddes and Patten (1958), in an attempt to improve the accuracy of death time estimation. The bodies were of varying stature, weight, and clothing cover and the time of death was known precisely. The environmental temperature varied between 40°F (4.4°C) and 70°F (21.1°C). The authors recorded the rectal and atmospheric temperatures at intervals, initially with a standard thermometer but later with an electrical continuous recording apparatus. They arbitrarily presumed that the rectal temperature at death was 99.0°F (37.2°C) and they confirmed the exponential fall in temperature but with considerable variation in the rate of cooling of each body (a range of 0.9°F or 0.5°C per hour in a series of 20 bodies). They noted that for the first 12 hours after death the TSD conformed reasonably accurately to the formula stated by Glaister (1942) (see Eq. (2.1)). However, as a body approached within 7°F (4°C) of ambient temperature, further cooling became extremely slow and temperature recording was not accurate in determining the TSD by any formula which relied on only one temperature reading. They found that the time taken to reach ambient temperature was much longer than in previous studies, not uncommonly up to 60−70 hours. Fiddes and Patten (1958) therefore discarded the last 15% of the temperature difference between the rectal temperature at death and the prevailing atmospheric temperature and considered that the body had "virtually cooled" when it had fallen by 85% of the difference in time taken for the body temperature to fall from the rectal temperature at death to ambient temperature. They called this the virtual cooling time (VCT) and they justified the empirical use of the figure of 85% for the VCT because they had assumed a rectal temperature at time of death of 99°F rather than the normal body temperature of 98.4°F. The virtual temperature difference (VTD) at the time of death was defined as 85% of the total difference between the rectal temperature at death and atmospheric temperature. To overcome the fact that bodies cooled at different rates, the temperature fall recordings were noted as percentages of the VCT and VTD rather than in degrees and hours.

The VTD was then plotted in a graph against the VCT for 50 cases selected because they did not suffer from illnesses which would have greatly altered the temperature at death such as febrile illnesses, protracted deaths, or marked variations in environmental temperature after death. It was noted that there was an exponential correlation and a linear relationship was obtained when these figures were converted to logarithmic values. There was a slight flattening of the line initially which they suggested corresponded to the initial plateau commented on by Shapiro (1954). Fiddes and Patten suggested that this graph could be useful in estimating the early TSD regardless of body stature, clothing, or environmental temperature provided the body remained undisturbed and that two or more rectal temperature recordings were taken over a period of several hours. They did acknowledge that if the rectal temperature at death was considerably higher or lower than 99°F, deductions by their method would be misleading.

The 1960s: The Search for an Accurate Formula

In 1962, Thomas Marshall, a pathologist working in collaboration with F.E. Hoare, a physicist, published their work on estimating the time of death using a mathematical formula based on the recording of rectal temperatures (Marshall and Hoare, 1962). Marshall and Hoare considered Newton's law of cooling (Winterton, 1999), which states that the rate of heat loss from a hot object cooling in air is directly proportional to the excess of temperature of the object over that of its surroundings, inadequate to explain the rate of heat loss from a human body after death. The study was carried out on more than 100 bodies over a period of 7 years, in which the temperatures were taken in the same unheated room and in which the environmental temperature varied no more than 4°F (1–2°C) during the period of each body recording, although it varied somewhat with the seasons (4.4–10°C between Jan. and Mar. and 15.5–21.1°C between Jun. and Aug.). Because the environmental temperature varied so much they considered it unnecessary to use an elaborate temperature recording system, using instead mercury in glass thermometers sealed in copper cases. Acknowledging the fact that internal body temperatures from different parts of the body fluctuated, and the best that could be done to measure internal body temperature was from some part of it, Marshall and Hoare recorded serial temperatures from the closed axilla, 3–4 inches (7.6–10.2 cm) within the rectum, and under the liver via a stab wound below the right costal margin. Weight and height were recorded and each body was naked and insulated from the table surface by two sheets. Temperature recordings were taken half- to one-hourly until they had fallen below 70°F (21°C). Graphs were constructed to illustrate the temperature falls. The authors showed that temperature falls were regular but varied in the rate of fall from different sites. Liver temperatures were the highest, rectal temperatures slightly lower, and both fell at about the same rate but more slowly than the axillary temperature recordings which were the lowest and most rapid to fall. The influence of environmental temperature was demonstrated by placing a body in a room 8−10°F (4−5°C) higher than the temperature of the liver and the rectum, when it was found that the axillary temperature rose almost at once, but there was a delay of 1−2 hours before the liver and rectal temperatures rose. In some cases Marshall and Hoare noted a sharp rise in the rectal and liver temperatures occurring in the first half hour of the experiment, which they attributed to local cooling caused by the insertion of the thermometer but they cautioned against interpreting this temperature rise to continued heat production within the body after death. The cooling curves from the rectum and liver followed a sigmoid form with an initial plateau of slow cooling lasting up to 5 hours, followed by a rapid even fall of temperature and a final slow, gradual decrease in temperature until ambient temperature was reached, after about 30 hours. In contrast, the axillary temperature often rose steeply during the first half or one hour, attributed to a rise in temperature following the placement of the thermometer after opening the axilla to the surrounding lower air temperature.

The authors then proceeded mathematically to show that the cooling of a body did not follow Newton's law of cooling which assumes that the body is in temperature equilibrium and that temperature differences do not exist or are sufficiently small for their effects to be disregarded. However, temperature differences do exist within the human body and after death they may change, either rising or falling. If the body cooled according to Newton's law, the graphical representation would be a straight line of gradually reducing gradient. However it was known that the cooling curve followed a sigmoid pattern. Therefore Newton's law did not apply in the first 12 hours after death as the temperature maintained a plateau or even rose slightly. Marshall and Hoare attributed this to the development of temperature gradients between the internal body organs and the surface of the body. After about 12 hours the temperature then fell gradually and conformed more closely to Newton's law. It was also recognized that the rate of body cooling depended on body size and surface area.

The authors then proceeded to devise a complex formula containing two exponential terms to express the rate of cooling of different bodies:

$$B = (\theta)^\circ - \frac{C}{Z - p} \qquad (2.2)$$

B, C, Z, and p were constants for the corpse under observation. "B" was a measure of the cooling of the body if it had cooled according to Newton's law of cooling. The value of "C" was the excess of body temperature over its environment at the moment of death. "$(\theta)^{\circ}$" was the temperature at the start of observations, "Z" was the cooling factor which expressed the cooling proportional to the temperature excess of the body over its environment, and "p" determined the rate of increase of "Z." Marshall and Hoare claimed that this formula, used in the experimental data, reproduced the cooling observed in reality with considerable accuracy.

In a second paper by Marshall (1962a), the cooling formula was used to construct curves showing the theoretical cooling from the time of death, of any naked body lying in still air, at a uniform temperature, once the height, weight, and external temperature were known. Four constants were required to construct the formula which the author denoted as B, C, Z, and p. A size factor was calculated from the mass and surface area of the body and defined as being inversely proportional to build, its value increasing as the body became thinner or smaller. The cooling factor expressed the rate of cooling per degree temperature difference. The constant B depended on the value of p and its value was difficult to determine. From a study of the cooling curves of certain cases, an average value of p of 0.4 was eventually determined which enabled the value of B to be calculated. These constants were then used in the cooling formula to calculate the theoretical temperature differences at various times after death. When the environmental temperature was added it gave the theoretical body temperatures at these various times. This enabled a series of cooling curves to be constructed for bodies with size factors from 170°F to 280 and in environmental temperatures from 40°F to 75°F (4.4°C to 23.8°C) at 5°F (2.8°C) intervals. When constructed, the curves graphically illustrated the influence of ambient temperature, an average body with a size factor of 210 cooled 2.5 times faster in a room at 4.4°C compared to a room at 23.8°C. The influence of body size was less pronounced in its effect on body cooling; after 18 hours in a room at 23.8°C, an obese and a thin body would differ in temperature by 4.2°C but in a room at 4.4°C, the difference would be 9.7°C. Three sets of cooling curve graphs were constructed for size factors of 210, for an average sized body, 170 for an obese body, and 280 for a thin adult. These graphs could be used to read the time of death, if the rectal temperature and weight of the body were known. The curves reproduced the initial temperature plateau, or delay in cooling, which occurred after death and which depended on environmental temperature and body size. In all the curves constructed, the delay in body cooling was most evident at higher temperatures, and a body of greater size took longer to cool than a smaller-sized body in a room at the same temperature. A constant rate of cooling was least likely to occur in thin adults cooling in a hot environment. Once the initial delay had passed the rate of cooling progressively decreased, closely following the principle of Newton's law of cooling. As the body approached environmental temperature, after about 12 hours the rate of cooling became much slower. The prolonged time to reach room temperature was not shown on the cooling curves and for convenience Marshall invoked the previous concept of VCT to consider the body cooled, when it had fallen through 85% of its initial temperature (Fiddes and Patten, 1958). Regardless of the size of the body, it took the same time to cool to 85% of the initial temperature. However, the authors found that the complete *cooling time* of a body was determined by the size of the body and not by the room temperature, a heavy body taking on average longer than a light body, an obese body taking about 41 hours, an average sized body 28 hours, and a thin body 19 hours. The *rate of cooling* however was determined by the room temperature as well as by the size of the body. Any formula to predict the TSD would have no value unless both of these factors were taken into account.

Marshall constructed cooling curves with temperatures taken from under the liver but found that the rate of fall in temperature differed depending on where the thermometer was placed in the upper abdomen. The author also found that although the rate of cooling increased more quickly than in the rectum, it did not reach the same rate as in the rectum. The error rate over a period of hours would therefore be greater than if temperatures were taken from the rectum. For ease of access and accuracy of recordings, the rectum was found to be the best region of the body in which to record temperatures. Finally, cooling curves were constructed for clothed bodies and Marshall concluded that there was no fundamental difference in the cooling rate of clothed bodies from that of naked bodies, but that a larger study was required to confirm this.

A third paper by Marshall (1962b) critically reviewed the use of the cooling formula and standard cooling curves. While initially it seemed a simple matter to estimate the time of death from the appropriate curve after the rectal temperature, the height and weight of the body had been measured in ideal conditions; in practice there were too many factors which would modify the result. Firstly, the cooling curves were constructed for use with average cases, but small differences from the average value of the cooling factor and one of the constants could translate to a larger error when the final estimation of the TSD was calculated. Similarly, although the use of an average value for p of 0.4 gave no greater average error than when it was calculated, this error could still not be ignored. Secondly, the experiments to construct the cooling curves were carried out in a room with a constant temperature, but in practice the temperature could vary due to factors such as doors and windows opening, people's movements and their heat radiation, and bed clothes being removed from a body. The cooling curve of a body in such an environment could vary so much from a standard cooling curve as to preclude any comparison. A third source of error was to assume that every corpse at death had the same rectal temperature, but a survey of 2000 consecutive bodies admitted to Leeds City morgue found over 50 cases in which the rectal temperature was higher than would have been expected (Marshall, 1962b). When cases with a fever, or found with heavy bedclothes, were excluded, there still remained 28 bodies where the cause of the raised temperature could not be explained. This had the effect of displacing the curve up or down or altering its slope so significantly, that the final time of death would be altered, in one case by as much as 9.2 hours. By far the greatest source of error was the variable environment to which the individual bodies had been subjected. Finally, calculation of the size factor could be difficult, because the different positions in which each body was found could lead to different quantities of heat loss from each body. Therefore the size factor would be difficult to standardize and over a period of time the error in estimating the time of death would be magnified. For all these reasons the use of body temperature to estimate the time of death could never give consistently accurate results and must be accepted only as being approximate.

James and Knight published a study of 110 bodies in 1965, estimating the time of death based on the method of Marshall and Hoare (Knight and James, 1965). All bodies had been subjected to changed environmental conditions, had varying types of clothing, and the times of death, which varied from 20 minutes to 75 hours, were known but not by the examiners. Temperatures were taken from deep within the rectum and the temperature at death was assumed to be 37°C. The outdoor shade temperature at noon, the temperature at the time the body arrived in the morgue, and the previous locations of the bodies were recorded. Using these data, a group of arbitrary factors (1, 1.25, 1.5, 1.75, and 2) by which the fall in rectal temperature was multiplied were selected to obtain a first approximation of the number of hours since death depending on whether the average air temperature was 0°C, 5°C, 10°C, 15°C, or 20°C, respectively, above average environmental temperature. An example was given of a body in an assessed average air temperature of 10°C with a rectal temperature of 27°C. In that case the estimated TSD was $(37 - 27) \times 1.5 = 15$ hours. This estimation was then arbitrarily altered by the examiner to account for unusual body clothing or environmental temperature. Estimates of the time of death were all given to the quarter hour. The authors were aware that they had not strictly adhered to Marshall and Hoare's criteria. The TSD was correctly estimated in 11 bodies, underestimated in 57 and overestimated in 32. In 35 of 100 bodies the error rate was less than 10%, in 54 less than 30%, in 90 less than 40%, in 96 less than 50%, and in 2 it was 100%. James and Knight were unable to improve their results by making a series of temperature observations instead of one and they concluded that great accuracy would never be achieved in estimating the TSD but systematic research could well reduce the size of errors.

Shapiro (1965) reemphasized the importance of the initial postmortem temperature plateau, which he recognized as being caused by the temperature gradient between the central body core and the temperature of the immediate environment. He recognized that any estimation of the TSD must take into consideration the duration of this plateau and that Newton's law of cooling did not apply to a cooling human body. Shapiro also acknowledged the final prolonged cooling, which occurred as the cadaver reached within 7°F (4°C) of the environmental temperature and in recognizing that rules of thumb sometimes gave a reasonable approximation of the TSD, he nevertheless stated that any rule of thumb for the estimation of the TSD could only provide some degree of accuracy if used after the body had begun the rapid phase of cooling and before the prolonged final cooling phase. The difficulty was to determine when this intermediate period began and finished.

Joseph and Schickele (1970) stated that the cooling of a body was a complex process as a temperature gradient was established between the interior parts of the body and the body surface and not until cooling of the surface occurred did the interior temperature begin to fall. As the distances from different parts of the body's interior to the surface varied, it followed that the body cooled in an uneven manner and cooling could not be expressed by just one cooling curve. For this reason they suggested abandoning the rectum as the point at which body temperature was measured and instead measuring temperature from within the center of the torso and that the term "body cooling" should be replaced with the term "torso cooling." Rectal temperature only measured temperature at the area surrounding the placement of the thermometer and did not reflect temperature drop from any other area within the body core. The authors used the model of an infinite cylinder, which they defined as a cylinder, the ends of which were so far away from the point of measurement that any heat loss through the ends was negligible from the point of view of the measurement being made, and which would thus simulate a human body cooling. They did not believe that the use of any one formula for estimation of the TSD was useful. Instead, they computed a series of cooling curves which could be used for any given set of circumstances.

Marshall (1969) summarized the state of research by pointing out the inaccuracy of any formula for estimating body cooling based on a single exponential term. Such a formula assumed that body cooling was most rapid immediately after death and progressively fell to ambient temperature when, in reality, the temperature curve assumed a sigmoid form; cooling was very slow during the first 3–5 hours, was faster and fell steadily and progressively for 9–12 hours and did not slow and become progressively flatter until it approached ambient temperature after 12–15 hours. Such a cooling curve could only be represented mathematically by a formula containing a sum series of exponential terms; the more exponential terms in the series, the more complex the formula and, consequently, the more unwieldy it would be to use in practice. Marshall's opinion was that sufficient accuracy could be achieved with the use of the formula given in his earlier article (Marshall and Hoare, 1962):

$$\theta = B.e^{-Zt} + \frac{C}{Z-p}.e^{-pt} \tag{2.3}$$

θ = the temperature excess of the rectum over the environment at time t and B, Z, and p are constants for the corpse under observation. This formula was found to reproduce the initial slow rectal cooling and also took account of body size. Marshall stated that the formula had been found to be accurate for up to 18 hours after death and could also be used to construct the cooling curve of any corpse once its length, weight, and the environmental temperature were known. However, one of the constants, p, in the formula could only be estimated and this produced an error of $\pm$ ¾ hour by the time the PMI had reached 15 hours. The formula also assumed a constant environmental temperature, which rarely occurred, and any formula containing more than two exponential terms (constants) would be unwieldy to use. The rectal temperature at death was unknown and temperature measurements were rarely taken in the same conditions of cooling which prevailed before the body was found. These factors meant that no cooling formula would produce consistently accurate estimates of the TSD and could be no more than an investigative guide.

The 1970s to Early 1980s: Continuing the Search for an Accurate Formula

Brown and Marshall (1974) continued to explore the use of a TSD formula and stated that one reason for the initial temperature plateau after death could be continuing metabolic processes but that in their view this was an insignificant factor. It was more likely due to the thermal conductivity and thermal capacity of the body producing a complex heat gradient. By a series of mathematical equations they explained why an equation with two exponential terms was adequate to explain the PMI, but they were still unable to improve the accuracy of estimation and no examples of its use were given.

A new approach was adopted by Simonsen et al. (1977) when they took postmortem temperature measurements in 20 cadavers, in whom the time of death was known with certainty to within

15 minutes, from the brain, calf muscle, liver, axilla, and rectum, as well as the environmental temperature. A thermoelectric thermometer with six electrodes was used to record temperatures from the various organs continuously and simultaneously. No attempt was made to create uniform environmental conditions as the purpose was to find an easy and practical method of estimating the TSD and a reliable site of temperature measurement. Measurements began between 30 minutes and 4.5 hours after death and lasted until the bodies had reached ambient temperature, which varied from 16.5 to 110 hours. Graphs of the cooling curves from each location were produced. The cooling curves from the rectum, axilla, and liver resembled an exponential curve with an initial plateau and long final cooling period, but the brain and calf temperatures fell steadily without initial temperature plateaus. The range of variation in temperature drop was smallest for the rectum and brain and the drop in temperature was steepest for the brain and calf muscle as these latter two sites were most influenced by the environmental temperature, due to their position closer to the body surface. The other sites of measurement gave less reliable estimates of the TSD and none were reliable after 20 hours post mortem. Because brain temperature measurements showed the least variation within the first 20 hours after death, they suggested that this might be the most useful organ to use for temperature measurement to estimate the TSD. However, if the brain temperature exceeded 25°C, the error in estimating the time of death would be 2.5 hours but, if brain temperature was below 25°C, the error would increase to about 5 hours. Even though brain temperature measurements showed the least variation, they were nevertheless so wide that this fact alone invalidated brain temperature measurement as a method of estimating TSD. The authors concluded that the variation in the temperature at the time of death in the cadavers was the crucial point in determining the TSD and that as all the methods of determination proposed so far were dependent on chemical processes, which were temperature-dependent, this variation was an insoluble problem. Finally, they conceded that attempts to estimate the time of death could never be more than an approximation.

Olaisen (1979) carried out a study of five cadavers in whom the time of death was known and in which temperature measurements began between 2 and 10 hours after death. The temperature at death was assumed to be 37°C and the rate of fall in temperature was uniform and rapid after an initial small plateau of about 2 hours which Olaisen attributed to the influence of brain size and of hair and clothing delaying cooling. The number of cases was small and the rate of fall varied from case to case, but Olaisen nevertheless concluded that measuring the rate of fall of brain temperature, after the initial temperature plateau, provided a more accurate method of temperature measurement than that from the rectum because clothing, body stature, and weight, which caused variability in temperature measurements from the latter site, did not need to be taken into consideration in estimating the time of death. By contrast Al-Alousi and colleagues (2002a), using microwave thermography, found brain temperature approached that of the environment after about 15 hours and that the cooling curve was steep. Therefore the use of brain temperature was applicable only for the first few hours, but liver and rectal temperature fall could be used for a longer period, as temperature fall was slower in these sites.

Green and Wright (1985a,b) devised a "time-dependent z equation" or TDZE method to try to improve the accuracy of estimation. They acknowledged that different bodies cooled at different rates, but pointed out that the general manner was the same for all bodies, that is, an initial lag period followed by a steep linear fall and then a slow exponential fall in temperature. The relative length of these periods varied with body build and clothing, a naked emaciated body cooling much faster than a clothed obese body. The aim of the TDZE method was to calculate the PMI using temperature data alone, which was possible if the gradient of the cooling curve and the extent by which the rectal temperature had fallen were known. This depended on the measurement of two rectal temperatures about 1 hour apart, reference to a single standard curve and a simple mathematical equation. Green and Wright avoided the use of body parameters because previous research using these measurements had been done in standard conditions with naked bodies lying flat on their backs, whereas in practice bodies cooled in different positions, different environments, and clothed and naked. Two measurements of rectal temperature were required as well as three temperature-related parameters; the temperature gradient (the fall in temperature per degree Centigrade per hour), the difference between rectal and ambient temperatures, and a measurement which they called the "reduced theta" or "θR," which was a measure of the extent by which the rectal temperature had fallen. The rectal temperature at death was arbitrarily fixed at 37.6°C. Green and Wright calculated θR, which they defined as the fractional drop in rectal temperature, by the following equation:

$$\theta R = \frac{\text{Rectal temperature at death} - \text{Measured rectal temperature}}{\text{Rectal temperature at death} - \text{Measured ambient temperature}}$$

(2.4)

The authors devised a "Reference Curve" with an explanation of how the TSD could be calculated from an equation. They analyzed 67 postmortem cases with an error rate of 30% at 3 hours after death and an increased error rate at 23 hours which they attributed to the slower rate of temperature fall as the bodies approached ambient temperature. These results were only marginally better than those of Marshall (1962b) and of Henssge (1979, 1981), who had reported results of his method in German. It therefore offered no improvement on these methods. Nokes et al. (1985) emphasized that the sigmoid shape of the cooling curve was the basis for all postmortem temperature investigations but all models to date had failed to take into account this plateau which they speculated could be partly caused by continuing glycogenolysis after death producing heat. However it was important to take into account environmental temperature, surface insulation of the body, and body size when assessing the early postmortem cooling of the body as these factors were responsible for maintaining the temperature plateau for up to 6 hours after death.

The Later 1980s: Henssge's Nomogram, a Definitive Mathematical Expression of TSD

Claus Henssge (1988) published a seminal study in English, in which he outlined a method of determining the approximate time of death from a single rectal temperature by reading it from a computed nomogram. The study had first been reported in German (Henssge, 1979, 1981). In the 1988 paper the results of 10 years' experience of using the method were also reported. A nomogram is a diagram representing a relationship between three or more variables by means of a number of straight or curved scales, so arranged that the value of one variable can be found by a simple geometrical construction, for example, by means of one or more straight lines drawn to intersect the scales at the appropriate values (Fig. 2.2).

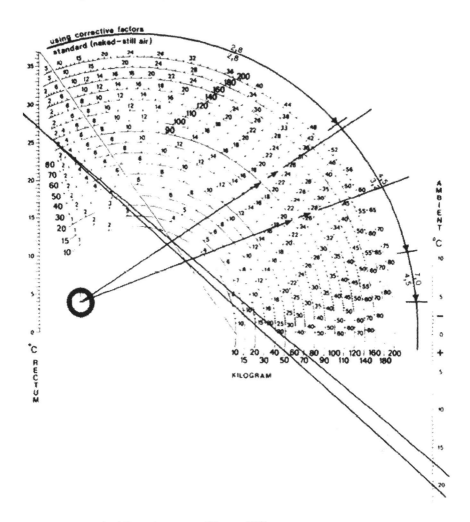

Figure 2.2 An example of Henssge's nomogram (Henssge, 1988).

Henssge's method was based on the two exponential equations developed by Marshall and Hoare (1962), the observations that the cooling of a body was a physical process and that the influence of biological factors such as fever, hypothermia, postmortem heat production, and of physical factors such as body build and composition, were either negligible or easily recognizable and could be accounted for. The method was based on a single rectal temperature measurement taken at least 8 cm within the rectum and the result was readily available at a scene of crime.

Henssge fixed the rectal temperature at time of death at 37.2°C, even if there was a fever. He defined the standard conditions of cooling as relating to a naked body lying extended on its back, on a thermally indifferent base in still air and in a closed room without any sources of heat radiation. He incorporated various constants into his calculations. Constant A described the postmortem temperature plateau and despite the rectal temperature at death being unknown and the duration of the plateau varying between 5 and 14 hours, Henssge found that there was a significant relationship between the duration of the plateau and the rate of temperature fall after the plateau. He calculated the value of constant A as being 1.25 in ambient temperatures up to 23°C and 1.11 in ambient temperatures above 23°C. Constant B related to the body weight to the power of -0.625 and Henssge calculated its value from a simple equation. The quantity of fatty tissue did not have any apparent influence on the value of B; neither did a calculation of body build based on the size factor which included surface area.

Using these constants, the value of Q, named the "standardized temperature" was calculated. Q was considered a good measure of the progress of cooling as Henssge's opinion was that errors of computed time of death should not be plotted against the progress of death time but against the progress of cooling. Using a value of Q as 1 at death and 0 when the rectal temperature had reached ambient temperature, Henssge found that in ambient temperatures between 5°C and 22°C the error range for estimation of the TSD fell into three groups. At the 95% confidence interval, for values of Q between 1 and 0.5 the error rate was ± 2.8 hours. For values of Q between 0.5 and 0.3 it was ± 3.2 hours and for values of Q between 0.3 and 0.2 the error rate was ± 4.5 hours. Large errors were found below a value of Q of 0.2 which corresponded to the prolonged cooling period before actual ambient temperature was reached and the estimation of the TSD with these values of Q was not possible.

Studies were then carried out on bodies in different environments, clothed and naked, in still and moving air. It was concluded that the clothed body cooled like a naked body that was 1.4 times heavier and that even a slight but permanent air movement accelerated the cooling of a naked body significantly. Empiric "corrective factors," based on the fact that a body with coverings would cool with a corrective factor greater than 1, that is, slower, while a body cooling in accelerated conditions would cool with a corrective factor less than 1. Using the corrective factors, error statistics for the estimation of the TSD were calculated for the three levels of the value of Q, that is, 1 to 0.5, 0.5 to 0.3, and 0.3 to 0.2. Corrective factors were also calculated for bodies in still and flowing water.

In actual casework, Henssge stated that his equations only gave an approximate value of death time. He devised a computer program (not detailed) and a series of nomograms to be used at the scene of a crime on a handheld Hewlett Packard 71B computer. The ambient temperature was calculated as the sum of the average daily temperatures from the time of death, as recorded by the nearest local weather station. The choice of corrective factor for body weights required judgment and experience and was only an approximation. He suggested choosing both an upper limit and a lower limit for the value of the corrective factor. Two lines could then be drawn on the nomogram, the first between rectal temperature and ambient temperature on the vertical scales on either side of the semicircular nomogram, and the second from a central point to the value of the corrective factor on the periphery of the semicircle. The TSD was then given as the value where the lines crossed on the nomogram. If there was a range of ambient temperature and an error range of corrective factors, four lines would be drawn giving an approximate range of the time of death where the four lines crossed (Fig. 2.2).

There were certain conditions where the method could not be used as the error would be too great and these were where there was strong radiation of heat or cold, where there had been hypothermia, where the place that the body had been found was not the same as the place of death, where there had been uncertain or severe changes in the cooling conditions between the time of death and the examination of the body and in unusual cooling conditions without any experience of a corrective factor. Special problems were discussed; Henssge had no experience in estimating the TSD found in temperatures above 23°C and so the nomograms did not take such temperatures into account. In bodies dying with a fever the temperature was often above 37.2°C which was the temperature at death assumed by the calculations for the nomogram method. Therefore a body with a temperature above this level would be considered to be still alive. For example, if the temperature was 40.2°C, the error in estimating the TSD would be

4 hours. As the temperature fell increasingly, the error rate fell into the acceptable range of 2–2.5 hours. In conditions where there had been movement of the body prior to assessment, the ambient temperature changes introduced an unacceptable error into the assessment of the TSD.

Finally, Henssge compared the nomogram method with other methods proposed to that date. A clear advantage was shown against using the rule of thumb method and the percentage method of Fiddes and Patten (1958). This latter method suffered from the disadvantage of not taking into account the temperature plateau. The nomogram method relied on one temperature measurement, whereas the methods of De Saram (De Saram et al., 1955), Fiddes and Patten (1958), Marshall (Marshall and Hoare, 1962; Marshall, 1962a) and Green and Wright (1985a,b) were based on measuring the slope of the drop in temperature by two or more temperature measurements at intervals. Henssge compared the nomogram method with all these methods and the results were not as accurate as the nomogram method. Green and Wright's (1985a,b) method fared worst. There were two reasons for these larger errors. Firstly, there was only a small decrease in the rectal temperature in the space of 1 hour, especially if the body was clothed. Therefore only a small mismeasurement in either temperature would translate into a large error when the TSD was calculated. Secondly, the measured rate of rectal temperature decrease was only valid for the cooling conditions during the period of temperature measurement. If the cooling conditions had been changed before or during measurement, large errors could be expected. Commenting on the part of the body from which temperature was recorded, Henssge stated that the radial distance from the body core and the position of the recording thermometer determined the actual temperature at any one time; the smaller the radius, the steeper the temperature fall. This was the reason for a more exact estimation of TSD from brain recordings but it was important to standardize the location. Henssge reported encouraging results in estimating the TSD during the early postmortem period by combining brain and rectal temperatures. Up to 6.5 hours brain temperatures gave a more precise estimate. From 6.5 to 10.5 hours after death, combining brain and rectal temperatures were more accurate and later than 10.5 hours post mortem, rectal temperatures were most accurate (Henssge et al., 1984).

CONTEMPORARY RESEARCH FROM 1988 TO THE PRESENT TIME

Since the publication by Claus Henssge of the nomogram method of estimating the TSD, most relevant research has been carried out by Claus Henssge and researchers in Germany and by Louay M. Al-Alousi from Glasgow. This research will be detailed together with other relevant work carried out contemporaneously.

As a follow up to the paper which introduced the nomogram method (Henssge, 1988), Henssge et al. (1988) proposed that the error in estimating the TSD might be reduced by combining all other objective measurements of time-related measurements of the TSD with the nomogram method. These were rigor mortis, livor mortis, mechanical and electrical excitability of skeletal muscle, and chemical excitability of the iris. Instead of taking the mean of these measurements they suggested taking the upper and lower limits, which would then be combined in a chart to estimate the TSD. However, no results using this approach were presented.

Henssge continued to experiment with dummies simulating human bodies and he formulated an extensive list of corrective factors to be used with bodies of different weight and with different types of clothing in different ambient temperature conditions (Henssge, 1992). These corrective factors were to be used with the nomogram method, in order to attempt to reduce the error in estimation of the TSD. No examples of the use of these corrective factors in actual practice were presented.

Althaus and Henssge (1999) carried out experiments with vulcanized rubber-coated cylinders filled with gel, simulating human bodies in order to determine whether the nomogram method was applicable where bodies had cooled in a high environmental temperature and then been moved to a lower temperature and vice versa. Two dummies were constructed to simulate bodies of 58.7 and 24.6 kg weight and heated to a body temperature of 37°C. Central core temperatures of the dummies and ambient temperatures were then measured, firstly, as they were cooled for a fixed period at 21°C ambient temperature and then moved rapidly to a cool room with an ambient temperature of 4°C for several hours. Secondly, the dummies, heated to 37°C, were stored at 4°C for several hours and then heated to 21°C ambient temperature. In the first series of experiments where the dummies were cooled, a second plateau in the cooling phase was noted, shorter than the initial plateau, as the dummies cooled to a lower ambient temperature. The cooling curve could be explained mathematically with a three-step procedure based on the two exponential term equation of Marshall and Hoare (1962) with an acceptable error range. However, in the second series of experiments where the dummies were heated from a lower temperature, rapidly more than 15°C, the two exponential term equation was unsuitable to describe the body cooling mathematically. This was attributed to heat flows in opposite directions; the cooled superficial layers would be reheated from outside and at the same time would be cooled by the lower temperature of the deeper layers. Althaus and Henssge concluded that the nomogram method was inapplicable in bodies cooled firstly for a long period in a low ambient temperature and after that subjected to a period in a higher ambient temperature.

Henssge and colleagues (2000a) published the results of the use of the nomogram in estimating the TSD in 72 cases over a 4-year period. In 61 of 67 cases where the method could be used, the estimated TSD fell within the 95% confidence limit. In 60 cases where the time could be verified exactly by other methods, the estimated TSD by the nomogram method matched exactly the TSD in 50 cases and partially in 10 cases. Problems arising in estimation of the TSD were discussed: one was the subjective bias in choice of corrective factors but an even greater error could be made in evaluating the true mean ambient temperature. These errors could only be reduced by the correct use of the method and the greater experience of the examiner. If ambient temperature varied before the body was discovered a mean value might not reflect the true value. The method could not be used where the body had been transported from an unknown place to the place where it had been found. There had been no improvement in the error rates quoted by Henssge (1988) for these 72 cases since he had first proposed the nomogram method.

Henssge and colleagues (1988) then returned to a question raised by Henssge over a decade previously in order to examine the nomogram method and its use in combination with non-temperature-based methods (Henssge et al., 2000b). The same series of cases as in the previous study (Henssge et al., 2000a) were used to determine if any combination of methods could improve the estimation of the TSD. The non-temperature-based methods were livor mortis, rigor mortis, mechanical and electrical excitability of skeletal muscle, and chemical excitability of the iris. The non-temperature-based methods could be used with the nomogram method in 69 of the 72 cases. In 49 of the cases the use of non-temperature-based methods caused a reduction in the limits of the estimated TSD compared with the results of the nomogram method alone and also provided a TSD in 4 cases where the nomogram method could not be used. In 14 cases the non-temperature-based methods provided no improvement in the estimation of the TSD and in 6 cases they provided an improvement in only one of the limits of the estimated TSD. In 7 cases the non-temperature-based methods alone proved to be more accurate than the nomogram method. In 49 cases where the TSD could be accurately estimated from the police records alone, the use of non-temperature-based methods provided an improvement in estimation in 44 of the cases. Henssge and colleagues found that the non-temperature method which gave the greatest accuracy was the electrical excitability of facial muscles by impulses from electrodes inserted into the eyebrow. Improvements however were modest.

Althaus and Henssge (1999) had found that while the estimation of the TSD in the case of a sudden decrease of ambient temperature during the cooling phase was possible, the estimation of TSD was not possible if a sudden increase in temperature occurred. Bisegna and colleagues (2008), experimenting on dummies, calculated a complex four-step mathematical procedure to prove that this was possible within reasonable error limits.

A different approach to estimation of TSD was taken by Al-Alousi and his colleagues who published a series of papers from 1986 to 2001 researching the estimation of the TSD using microwave probes to measure body organ temperatures. A preliminary study on the use of microwave thermography in estimating the TSD had been carried out on 100 human fatalities (Al-Alousi and Anderson, 1986). In this initial study it was concluded that microwave thermography was useful in estimating the TSD, giving a similar degree of accuracy as other temperature-measuring devices. Cooling curves were produced for the brain, liver, and rectum which required triple exponential functions for their expression. The error rates were acceptable but the method was insufficiently precise to be used in legal evidence.

In a subsequent paper, the system and method of use were explained (Al-Alousi et al., 1994). Two flexible microwave probes were placed on the skin of the temporal region to measure brain temperature and on the skin of the right hypochondrium to measure liver temperature. Two rigid thermocouples measured environmental and rectal temperatures. The thermocouples were attached to a microwave radioreceiver and a data logger which measured and computed the temperature data. Thermal radiation consists of centimetric or microwave, millimetric and infrared waves. Microwave penetration was the less penetrative part of thermal radiation from body tissues and the microwave probe was designed to magnify and record this wavelength. The greater the water content of tissue, the less was the microwave penetration. Penetration through fat and bone was greater than through muscle and skin. The probes placed on the skin were designed to overcome the refraction back into the body of microwaves when they reached the skin/air boundary. The temperature resolution of the system was $0.1°C$ and the response time was 2 seconds. The accuracy of temperature measurement of all the probes was $±0.6°C$. The penetration depth of the microwave probes was 1.6 cm in high water content tissue and 10 cm in low water content tissue, which was sufficient to measure the interior temperatures of the liver and brain.

The system was assessed by measuring brain and liver temperatures in 14 living healthy subjects and 5 cadavers. In addition, the temperatures of the tissues of the cadavers in the right hypochondrium were measured at different depths (skin, subcutaneous tissues, muscle, and liver) by inserted thermocouples. Calibration of the probes using glycerol and comparison with a mercury thermometer and thermocouple was successful. Temperature readings given by the microwave probes depended on the temperature of the tissues and the degree of microwave attenuation, which in turn was determined by the type of tissue traversed. There was no difference in attenuation between living and dead tissues and the authors concluded that the microwave thermography system offered an accurate technique to measure the temperature of internal body organs by a non-invasive and more ethically acceptable method.

Continuing this line of research, Al-Alousi and colleagues (2002a) studied 117 cadavers. These were taken as soon as possible after death to a morgue where microwave recordings of brain, liver, and rectal temperatures were undertaken, as the cadavers cooled for up to 60 hours after death. The rectal and environmental temperatures were recorded with electrical thermocouples, the liver and brain temperatures with microwave probes. Data were recorded on a data logger and then analyzed with the use of a reference graph, a reference chart ruler, or computer software (type not stated). The temperatures of the brain, liver, and rectum at the time of death were determined by measuring the temperatures for the first 3 hours, fitting them to a curve, and then extrapolating the temperatures from the different organs backwards over the PMI. A temperature difference ratio (R) was calculated from the temperature at each of these specific body sites at a given time, the temperature of the environment at that same time and the temperature of these specific body sites at the moment of death. Curve-fitting procedures were then calculated for the values of temperature differences versus PMI using a triple exponential equation. Al-Alousi and colleagues concluded that postmortem cooling was a complicated phenomenon, unable to be described by a simple model, and that the best description was by triple exponential equations. There were differences between body sites with respect to the rate of cooling and between covered and naked bodies. The rectum as a site for temperature recording was flawed because it had a higher temperature than other body sites and standard placement for temperature recording was difficult. Brain and liver recordings were more representative of body cooling.

In a second part of the study using the same 117 bodies, the authors modified the computer software for use in the field (Al-Alousi et al., 2001). The computer software was not specified but the authors stated that it could be obtained by a special arrangement with them. Temperature difference ratios (R) were calculated for selected values of rectal and environmental temperatures from 1°C to 36°C. Thirty-six curves were compiled to represent the relationship between the rectal and the environmental temperatures over the temperature range of 1−36°C. The curves were then plotted to match the average rectal cooling curves for both covered and naked bodies, thus producing a reference chart ruler. Further calculation incorporated an error range of ±1 standard deviation. To use the system in the field, the temperature of a body site and the temperature of the environment were recorded, which enabled the value of R to be read from the reference chart ruler. Using this value, the PMI, ± 1 standard deviation, could then be read from curves for either naked or clothed bodies.

Al-Alousi and colleagues continued their research on the same 117 bodies and published three more studies (Al-Alousi et al., 2002a,b; Al-Alousi, 2002). Two studies discussed the factors influencing the precision of estimating the PMI using the triple exponential formula. In the first study, the bodies were separated into naked and covered groups and fat and thin groups (Al-Alousi et al., 2002a). The separation into "fat" or "thin" depended on a formula based on surface area and weight which gave a "cooling size factor." Using this cooling size factor they found that thin bodies cooled faster than fat ones, but only in 56% of cases. The correlation between the rate of body cooling and body build was strong and age had no influence on the rate of cooling. In most cases covered bodies cooled more slowly than naked ones. Brain cooling was found to approach environmental temperature faster than the liver and rectum. The liver was the slowest to cool in the covered group and the rectal cooling was intermediate. They concluded that there was no single body parameter which could be used to quantifiably predict the cooling behavior in all cases, but covering the torso significantly slowed the rate of body cooling. In the second study, the effect of the body temperature at the moment of death on the postmortem cooling rate was studied in order to incorporate this in the triple exponential formula (Al-Alousi et al., 2002b). Temperature measurements for the brain, liver, and rectum were taken every 5–10 minutes after the body entered the morgue. The temperatures of these organs at the moment of death were determined by fitting the temperature data for the first 3 hours to single exponential equations to form fitted curves which were then extrapolated backwards by regression analysis. The mean time between death and the start of monitoring was 32 ± 15 minutes, 74 (63.3%) cases were between 15 and 45 minutes and only 2 cases started after a period of 3 hours after death. Environmental temperatures ranged between 8.38°C and 22.76°C (mean value was 15.2 ± 3.2°C). A factor was calculated and incorporated in the triple exponential formula to allow determination of the temperature at death from the temperature of any organ but temperatures from the brain and liver had to be taken with the microwave probe. Al-Alousi and colleagues determined that if the temperature of the environment was kept constant, the body temperature at the moment of death would determine the temperature gradient between the body and its surrounding medium. Thus a higher temperature at death would mean a steeper rate of cooling and a greater amount of heat to be lost to bring the body to equilibrium with the environmental temperature. The various conditions causing temperature variations at the moment of death were discussed. From their calculations they theorized that if the same body was allowed to cool twice, starting from a different body temperature, the time required to reach equilibrium would be the same although the rate of cooling would not be constant at all stages. They conceded, however, that this would be impossible to verify.

Finally, Al-Alousi (2002) studied the shapes of the brain, liver, and rectal cooling curves and compared them in naked and covered bodies. In the covered group the liver had the most rapid and the brain the slowest cooling rates at 6 hours post mortem, while at 12 hours the brain was slowest and the rectum the most rapid. In the naked group, the rectum cooled slowest and the brain the most rapid at 6 hours post mortem, but at 12 hours the brain had the slowest rate of cooling. In the naked group, in all sites, cooling was faster than in the covered group. On average, thin bodies cooled faster than obese bodies. The initial temperature plateau was found in only 22% of bodies, the rectum in the naked group having the highest incidence of a plateau (27%) compared with 7% for the brain and liver curves. The rectum was the only site where a significant temperature plateau occurred, irrespective of body weight and the presence or absence of clothing. Al-Alousi concluded that the cooling curve was of a compound type and that the rate of cooling was not uniform throughout the whole PMI.

The work of Al-Alousi and his colleagues demonstrated that because of the non-uniformity of body cooling and the fact that the body temperature at the moment of death could not be known, the estimation of the TSD could never be exact.

Nokes and colleagues (1992) compared eight methods of estimating the TSD on eight cadavers in which the time of death was known. The methods were two rules of thumb using rectal temperature measurement:

$$TSD = \frac{(\text{Temperature at death} - \text{Temperature when found})}{1.5} \qquad (2.5)$$

TSD = (Temperature at death − Temperature when found) + 3   (2.6)

Also compared were De Saram's method (De Saram et al., 1955), the method of Fiddes and Patten (1958), Marshall and Hoare's (1962) method, Green and Wright's (1958a,b) method, Al-Alousi and Anderson's method (Al-Alousi et al., 2001), and the nomogram method of Henssge (1988). In two cadavers the TSD was underestimated by all methods and very large errors were produced by Al-Alousi and Anderson's and Fiddes and Patten's methods on one cadaver and on average the second rule of thumb, that of Knight (1991), produced the best results in all cadavers. Nokes and colleagues stressed that this was a small study, but it appeared that the increasingly complex mathematical methods offered no increased accuracy over simple rules of thumb.

OTHER STUDIES ATTEMPTING TO IMPROVE THE ESTIMATION OF TSD

Other approaches seeking to improve the TSD estimation are briefly explored in this final section.

Nokes et al. (1983) presented a cooling model based on four rectal temperatures, an estimated body core temperature at time of death of 37°C, and the environmental temperature, postulating that if the environmental temperature varied by no more than 2°C it had no effect on the rectal temperature curve due to the poor conducting properties of the body. They used computer software and based the calculations on the equation of Brown and Marshall (1974) to estimate the PMI on eight bodies. The error rate in estimating the TSD was within 51 minutes of the actual time of death for the case histories presented.

Morgan and colleagues (1988) presented a method of estimating the PMI without prior knowledge of the body temperature at death, the size of the body, or the original environmental temperature. Temperature measurements were taken simultaneously by means of thermocouples placed in both middle ears and on the skin of the forearm and thigh. The measurements were then incorporated in an algorithm. Observations were taken only from three corpses and although the authors stated that it was intended to further develop the technique, no follow-up studies on the use of the method are known to have been carried out.

Niels Lynnerup (1993) presented a computer software program using algorithms based on the cooling formula devised by Marshall and Hoare. Lynnerup claimed that the program could overcome the uncertainties related to ambient temperature and rectal temperature at death and give a better estimation of the TSD. However the study did not present the practical use of the program on corpses and no follow-up studies on this method seem to have been presented.

A different approach was adopted by Baccino and colleagues (1996), who studied a series of 138 cadavers subdivided into four groups according to the ambient temperature between 0°C and 23°C (0−5°C, 6−10°C, 11−15°C, 16−23°C), at which they were stored while cooling. The mean of the tympanic membrane temperature in both outer ears was measured on each cadaver and the rectal temperature, 8 cm inside the rectum, was also recorded on each cadaver. The authors suggested that measuring the temperature from the tympanic membrane provided a more accurate representation of the fall in temperature of the inner body core than did the rectum, as it was recorded from a site where there was an absence of clothing or of intervening organs. The cooling curve was also more linear without the initial plateau. Their aim was to try to improve the accuracy of TSD estimation, but to keep the method simple. To do this they proposed combining biochemical methods and temperature measurement methods. They theorized that environmental temperature affected body temperature measurement methods, resulting in an underestimation of the TSD, while heat-generating cytolytic processes were speeding up the process of decomposition and overestimating the TSD. By combining the methods they hoped to improve the estimation of TSD.

Using multivariate regression analysis, they compared two rule-of-thumb methods of measuring TSD with Henssge's nomogram and also with the estimation of plasma electrolytes, CSF, and vitreous humor potassium levels. Baccino and colleagues in comparing methods using outer ear temperatures with the same methods using rectal temperatures, found that outer ear temperature measurements correlated better with TSD than did rectal temperature measurements. One rule of thumb method, Eq. (2.6) (Knight, 1991), proved to be superior to the other, Eq. (2.5) (Glaister, 1942; Rentoul and Smith, 1973; Clark et al., 1997), as well as Henssge's nomogram at estimating the TSD. The use of vitreous humor potassium measurement was the next best method of measuring TSD, but plasma and CSF electrolyte measurements were inaccurate methods. A combination of methods proved better than any single method.

In discussing the results, Baccino and colleagues cautioned against using the method of measuring outer ear temperature when there was blood in the ear canal or when the body had been lying on one side with one ear in close contact with a surface. It should also not be used where the PMI was greater than 15 hours as the error of estimation increased greatly after this time. They developed a formula which encompassed all temperature subgroups. Rutty (1997) criticized the use of the outer ear canal as a source of temperature measurement, implying that the method would be difficult to standardize. He stated that foreign material, blood, the shape of the canal, and position of the temperature probe, as well as the uncertain core temperature at death, could make temperature measurement inaccurate. One of the authors, Baccino (1997), in reply defended the method, stating that all placements of the thermometer in the outer ear canal were standardized.

Yet another algorithm based on an averages-based method of short-term PMI estimation using a graphing calculator and spreadsheet program, was presented by Eric Nelson (2000). Nelson used data provided by Nokes and colleagues (1992) to calculate an absolute relative error (ARE) by dividing the absolute value of the difference between the actual PMI and the estimated PMI by the actual PMI. By using this ARE, he compared his method with eight other methods and found his method to be more accurate. The ARE for Nelson's method was 0.05 (SD of 0.05) over 24 hours while the next most accurate methods were a rule-of-thumb method (Eq. (2.4)) with an ARE of 0.16 (SD of 0.7) over 10 hours and Marshall and Hoare's (1962) method with an ARE of 0.20 (SD of 0.11) over 10 hours. No follow-up studies using this method appear to have been published.

Finally, Mall and colleagues in 2004 studied 35 bodies after admission to a medicolegal institute where they were kept at a constant environmental temperature for 12−36 hours (Mall et al., 2005). The times of death were known exactly but the environmental temperatures at the time of death were not known. The aim of the study was to develop a mathematical formula incorporating an additional factor to account for the unknown temperature at time of death. Cooling curves were constructed which gave an acceptable error rate of ±4 hours over 12−36 hours. This error rate compared favorably with the error rate quoted by Henssge (1988) of ±2.5 hours up to 11 hours post mortem with known environmental conditions.

CONCLUSION

The investigation of estimating the TSD by temperature-based methods has produced an extensive literature in the past 200 years. Several important milestones are noteworthy since Dr John Davy (1839) recognized that measurement of body temperature while it cooled after death could lead to an estimation of the PMI. Taylor and Wilks (1863) noted the initial temperature plateau after death in the cooling curve and Rainy (1868) was the first to note that cooling of a body did not follow Newton's law of cooling.

In the 20th century, Shapiro (1954) recognized the sigmoid shape of the cooling curve, while Marshall and Hoare (Marshall, 1962b) in the 1960s confirmed the complex nature of body cooling and the necessity of defining it mathematically with a formula if any accuracy in determining the time of death in the early stages was to be attained. In the 1980s Claus Henssge (Henssge, 1979; Nokes et al., 1985) developed his nomogram method and subsequently refined it. Although this seems to be the most accurate method at the present time there is still an error rate of 2−4 hours during the first 12 hours or so after death.

REFERENCES

Al-Alousi, L.M., 2002. A study of the shape of the post-mortem cooling curve in 117 forensic cases. Forensic Sci. Int. 125, 237−244.

Al-Alousi, L.M., Anderson, R.A., 1986. Microwave thermography in forensic medicine. Police Surg. 30, 30−42.

Al-Alousi, L.M., Anderson, R.A., Land, D.V., 1994. A non-invasive method of post-mortem temperature measurements using a microwave probe. Forensic Sci. Int. 64, 35−46.

Al-Alousi, L.M., Anderson, R.A., Worster, D.M., Land, D.V., 2001. Multiple probe thermography for estimating the post-mortem interval: part II. Practical versions of the triple exponential formulae (TEF) for estimating the time of death in the field. J. Forensic Sci. 46 (2), 323–327.

Al-Alousi, L.M., Anderson, R.A., Worster, D.M., Land, D.V., 2002a. Factors influencing the precision of estimating the post-mortem interval using the triple-exponential formulae (TEF) part I. A study of the effect of body variables and covering of the torso on the post-mortem brain, liver and rectal cooling rates in 117 forensic cases. Forensic Sci. Int. 125, 223–230.

Al-Alousi, L.M., Anderson, R.A., Worster, D.M., Land, D.V., 2002b. Factors influencing the precision of estimating the post-mortem interval using the triple-exponential formulae (TEF) part II. A study of the effect of body temperature at the moment of death on the post-mortem brain, liver and rectal cooling in 117 forensic cases. Forensic Sci. Int. 125, 231–236.

Althaus, L., Henssge, C., 1999. Rectal temperature time of death nomogram: sudden change of ambient temperature. Forensic Sci. Int. 99, 171–178.

Baccino, E., et al., 1996. Outer ear temperature and time of death. Forensic Sci. Int. 83, 133–146.

Baccino, E., 1997. Letter to the editor. Forensic Sci. Int. 83, 173.

Bisegna, P., Henssge, C., Althaus, L., Giusti, G., 2008. Estimation of the time since death: sudden increase of ambient temperature. Forensic Sci. Int. 176, 196–199.

Brown, A., Marshall, T.K., 1974. Body temperature as a means of estimating the time of death. Forensic Sci. 4, 125–133.

Burman, J.W., 1880. On the rate of cooling of the human body after death. Edinburgh. Med. J. 25, 993–1003.

Cairns, F.J., Forbes, J.A., 1952. Time since death. Med. J. Aust. 2 (17), 585–586.

Clark, M.A., Worrell, M.B., Pless, J.E., 1997. Post mortem changes in soft tissues. In: Haglund, W.D., Sorg, M.H. (Eds.), Forensic Taphonomy: The Post-mortem Fate of Human Remains. CRC Press, Boca Raton, p. 152. Ch. 9.

Davy, J., 1839. Observations on the temperature of the human body after death. Researches Physiological and Anatomical Vol. I. Smith, Elder and Co., London, pp. 228–248.

De Saram, G.S.W., Webster, G., Kathirgamatamby, N., 1955. Post-mortem temperature and the time of death. J. Crim. Law Criminol. Police Sci. 46 (4), 562–577.

Fiddes, F.S., Patten, T.D., 1958. A percentage method for representing the fall in body temperature after death. J. Forensic Med. 5 (1), 2–15.

Glaister, J., 1942. Medical Jurisprudence and Toxicology, seventh ed. E & S Livingstone, Edinburgh, p. 119. Ch. 4.

Green, M.A., Wright, J.C., 1985a. Post-mortem interval estimation from body temperature data only. Forensic Sci. Int. 28, 35–46.

Green, M.A., Wright, J.C., 1985b. The theoretical aspects of the Time Dependent Z Equation as a means of post-mortem interval estimation using body temperature data only. Forensic Sci. Int. 28, 53–62.

Henssge, C., 1979. Precision of estimating the time of death by mathematical expression of rectal body cooling. Z. Rechtsmed. 83, 49–67.

Henssge, C., 1981. Estimation of death time by computing the rectal body cooling under various cooling conditions. Z. Rechtsmed. 87, 147–178.

Henssge, C., 1988. Death time estimation in case work I. The rectal temperature time of death nomogram. Forensic Sci. Int. 38, 209–236.

Henssge, C., 1992. Rectal temperature time of death nomogram: dependence of corrective factors on the body weight under stronger thermic insulation conditions. Forensic Sci. Int. 54, 51–56.

Henssge, C., et al., 2000a. Experiences with a compound method for estimating the time since death: I. Rectal temperature nomogram for time since death. Int. J. Legal Med. 113, 303–319.

Henssge, C., et al., 2000b. Experiences with a compound method for estimating the time since death: II. Integration of non-temperature-based methods. Int. J. Legal Med. 113, 320–331.

Henssge, C., Frekers, R., Reinhardt, S., Beckman, E.-R., 1984. Determination of time of death on the basis of simultaneous measurement of brain and rectal temperatures. Z. Rechtsmed. 93, 123–133.

Henssge, C., Madea, B., Gallenkemper, E., 1988. Death time estimation in case work II. Integration of different methods. Forensic Sci. Int. 39, 77–87.

Joseph, A.E.A., Schickele, E., 1970. A general method for assessing factors controlling post mortem cooling. J. Forensic Sci. 15, 364–391.

Knight, B., 1991. Post-mortem decomposition, Simpson's Forensic Medicine, 10th ed. Edward Arnold, London, p. 39. Ch. 3.

Knight, B.H., James, W.R.L., 1965. Errors in estimating the time of death. Med. Sci. Law 5, 111–116.

Lyle, H.P., Cleveland, F.P., 1956. Determination of the time of death by body heat loss. J. Forensic Sci. 1, 11–24.

Lynnerup, N., 1993. A computer program for the estimation of time of death. J. Forensic Sci. 38 (4), 816–820.

Mall, G., et al., 2005. Temperature based death time estimation with only partially known environmental conditions. Int. J. Legal Med. 119, 185–194.

Marshall, T.K., 1962a. Estimating the time of death: the use of the cooling formula in the study of post-mortem body cooling. J. Forensic Sci. 7 (2), 189–210.

Marshall, T.K., 1962b. Estimating the time of death: the use of body temperature in estimating the time of death. J. Forensic Sci. 7 (2), 211–221.

Marshall, T.K., 1969. The use of body temperature in estimating the time of death and its limitations. Med. Sci. Law 9, 178–182.

Marshall, T.K., Hoare, F.E., 1962. Estimating the time of death: the rectal cooling after death and its mathematical expression. J. Forensic Sci. 7 (1), 56–81.

Morgan, C., Nokes, L.D.M., Williams, J.H., Knight, B., 1988. Estimation of the post-mortem period by multiple site temperature measurements and the use of a new algorithm. Forensic Sci. Int. 39, 89–95.

Nelson, E., 2000. Estimation of short term post mortem interval utilising core body temperature: a new algorithm. Forensic Sci. Int. 109, 31–38.

Nokes, L.D.M., Brown, A., Knight, B., 1983. A self-contained method for determining time since death from temperature measurements. Med. Sci. Law 23 (3), 166–170.

Nokes, L.D.M., Hicks, B., Knight, B.H., 1985. The post- mortem temperature plateau – fact or fiction? Med. Sci. Law 25 (4), 263–264.

Nokes, L.D.M., Flint, T., Williams, J.H., Knight, B.H., 1992. The application of eight reported temperature – based algorithms to calculate the post-mortem interval. Forensic Sci. Int. 54, 109–125.

Olaisen, B., 1979. Post-mortem decrease in brain temperature. Z. Rechtsmed. 83 (3), 253–257, Article in German, abstract only.

Rainy, H., 1868. On the cooling of dead bodies as indicating the length of time that has elapsed since death. Glasgow. Med. J. 1, 323–330.

Rentoul, E., Smith, H., 1973. Timing of death. In: Rentoul, E., Smith, H. (Eds.), Glaister's Medical Jurisprudence and Toxicology, 13th ed. Churchill Livingstone, Edinburgh, pp. 132–133.

Rutty, G.N., 1997. Letter to the editor. Forensic Sci. Int. 87, 171–172.

Schwarz, F., Heidenwolf, H., 1953. Post mortem cooling and its relation to the time of death. Int. Police Crim. Rev. 73 (339), 339–344.

Shapiro, H.A., 1954. Medico-legal mythology: some popular forensic fallacies. J. Forensic Med. 1, 144–169.

Shapiro, H.A., 1965. The post-mortem temperature plateau. J. Forensic Med. 12 (Suppl.), 4, 137–141.

Simonsen, J., Voigt, J., Jeppeson, N., 1977. Determination of the time of death by continuous post mortem temperature measurements. Med. Sci. Law 17 (2), 112–121.

Taylor, A.S., Wilks, D., 1863. On the cooling of the human body after death. Guy's Hosp. Rep.180–211.

Underwood, E.A., 1951. The history of the quantitative approach in medicine. Br. Med. Bull. 7 (4), 265–274.

Vaughan, E.M., 1921. Method of determining approximate time of death. J. Am. Med. Assoc. 76 (9), 608–609.

Winterton, R.H.S., 1999. Newton's law of cooling. Contemp. Phys. 40 (3), 205–212.

Womack, F., 1887. The rate of cooling of the body after death. St. Bartholomew's Hosp. Rep. 23 (Suppl.), 193–200.

CHAPTER 3

Biochemical Methods of Estimating the Time Since Death

INTRODUCTION

The estimation of the postmortem interval (PMI) by biochemical means is based on the analysis of chemical substances which are released after death and accumulate in the body. In theory, if any

Human Body Decomposition. DOI: http://dx.doi.org/10.1016/B978-0-12-803691-4.00003-0

substance can be measured accurately and correlated with the time since death (TSD), it might provide a method of determining the PMI. Within a few minutes of death, autolysis, or cell disruption, begins with the release of water, of which the body is mainly composed, and enzymes, which begin the degradation of proteins, lipids, and carbohydrates. Water containing chemical breakdown products accumulates as blisters under the skin and intestinal cell walls break down, releasing bacteria which aid in the putrefaction process. Fungi and protozoa colonize body cavities, destroying and consuming body tissues. Proteins, lipids, and carbohydrates are broken down by the enzymes proteases, lipases, and glycogenase, respectively, into amino acids, triglycerides, and glucose. These last three substances are then broken down further into simpler molecules, electrolytes, and gas with the help of microorganisms. Amino acids finally break down to ammonia gas and amines such as histamine, tyramine, tryptamine, and phenylethylamine as well as the volatile amines, putrescine, and cadaverine (Forbes, 2008).

Triglycerides are further broken down by hydrolysis and the action of lipases to form saturated and unsaturated fatty acids. In aerobic conditions the unsaturated fatty acids are oxidized to form odoriferous aldehydes and ketones, but in anaerobic conditions the unsaturated fatty acids are hydrogenated to form saturated fatty acids which form a solid mass of adipocere tissue. Some of the fatty acids formed are volatile fatty acids such as propionic, butyric, and valeric acids. Measuring the ratio of these in the soil under a buried body may be useful in determining the TSD (Vass et al., 1992). Microorganisms break down carbohydrates to form glucose. Fungi may form organic acids such as glucuronic, oxalic, and citric acids. Oxalic acid has been found to be a useful determinant of the TSD (Vass et al., 2002). In an aerobic environment glucose will be broken down to lactic and pyruvic acids and then to carbon dioxide and water while in anaerobic conditions, butyric and acetic acids will be formed and then subsequently broken down to ethanol and butanol. Bacterial fermentation will produce methane, hydrogen sulfide, and hydrogen gases (Forbes, 2008).

A soup of fluid is therefore produced during decomposition which contains electrolytes and organic compounds. Theoretically, it should be possible to sample and measure some of these from various compartments of the body, in order to equate the concentrations with the TSD. Blood is unsuitable for sampling because it pools in the dependent parts of the body after death and clots. The variability of analytes in post-mortem blood and autolysis of blood cells and vascular endothelium is too rapid to be of practical use for obtaining chemical markers (Coe, 1993; Madea and Musshoff, 2007). Similarly, cells lining the subarachnoid space in the brain also undergo too rapid autolysis, such that variability in the chemical constituents limits the use of cerebrospinal fluid (CSF) for analysis (Naumann, 1959). Fluids such as the vitreous humor from the eye and synovial fluid from joints, which are located in closed compartments, have been found to be of more use in providing samples for chemical analysis because they are protected from bacterial action, chemical inter-action with other body breakdown products, and putrefaction for a longer period after death. The estimation of potassium in the vitreous humor has been studied in the postmortem period in detail (Naumann, 1959; Jaffe, 1962; Sturner and Gantner, 1964; Leahy and Farber, 1967; Lange et al., 1994; Tagliaro et al., 1999, 2001; Madea, 2005) and together with Henssge's nomogram (Henssge, 1988) are the methods employed most often to estimate the TSD in the early postmortem period.

CHEMICAL INVESTIGATION OF VITREOUS HUMOR

Determining Validity and Defining Methods of Collection and Measurement

In life, an active transport mechanism maintains chemical equilibrium between plasma potassium in the retinal vessels and the vitreous humor of the eye, but at death this ceases and potassium concentration in the vitreous humor increases due to simple diffusion from the retina and to a lesser extent, from the lens (Madea and Henssge, 2002). Because of the varying concentration throughout the globe of the eye, collection of vitreous humor should be standardized by aspirating all the vitreous with a large-gauge needle inserted through the outer canthus of both eyes into the center of the globe (Coe, 1993). To prevent contamination with retinal cells, high suction should not be applied and all the vitreous humor should be aspirated as there is variability between many of the solutes in the fluid next to the retina and the fluid in the center of the globe. Vitreous humor is viscid; it should be centrifuged and the supernatant fluid analyzed. Each laboratory should determine reference ranges of normality for the chemicals being analyzed. Most chemical investigations of vitreous humor have concentrated on postmortem concentrations of potassium, but more recently, hypoxanthine concentrations have been studied (Saugstad and Olaisen, 1978; Madea et al., 1994).

Naumann (1959) measured concentrations of urea, glucose, creatinine, chlorine, inorganic phosphate, calcium, sodium, and potassium in the postmortem vitreous humor. He compared concentrations of the same substances in postmortem CSF and found a greater rise in the concentrations in CSF compared with vitreous humor. The potassium concentration was twice the initial concentration in vitreous humor and seven times the initial concentration in CSF, 9 hours post mortem. This was attributed to the rapid autolysis of the ependymal cells lining the brain ventricles. Although Naumann noted the increase in potassium concentration in the vitreous humor after death he did not suggest it as a measure of the PMI. Jaffe (1962) was the first to do this when he estimated the potassium concentration at various intervals after death in the vitreous humor of 31 bodies in which the PMI was known. People dying with uremia or electrolyte abnormalities were excluded. A steady rise in potassium concentration from an initial level of 4 mEq/L up to 8 mEq/L after 9 hours was noted after which it rose more slowly, reaching a concentration of 10 mEq/L after 30 hours. It then continued to rise slowly up to 125 hours post mortem. A linear relationship between potassium concentration and the logarithm of the number of hours after death was noted. In discussing the results, Jaffe warned that excessive force of aspiration of vitreous fluid would detach retinal cells and result in falsely high potassium values. Jaffe also stated that withdrawal of small amounts of fluid rather than the whole amount also gave unrepresentative results, suggesting that the distribution of potassium throughout the vitreous fluid was not uniform. The levels of lactic acid, pyruvic acid, ascorbic acid, non-protein nitrogen, sodium, and chloride were also studied but found to be of less use than the measurement of potassium. This study stimulated research into using vitreous potassium concentration as a measure of the PMI.

Adelson and colleagues (1963) measured potassium concentrations in the vitreous humor of 349 eyes in 209 individuals who had died from multiple causes of trauma and disease. The time of death was known to within 15 minutes. There was no difference in potassium concentration from diluted or undiluted specimens, from the right or left eye, or by storing the samples for 4−5 days. They found that the potassium concentration increased in proportion to the increase in PMI, but, contrary to Jaffe's (1962) findings, the relationship was linear between potassium concentration and the PMI, not on a logarithmic scale but on an arithmetic scale. The type of death did not affect the slope of the regression line, its intercept, or the average potassium value, but the potassium concentration was more variable where the agonal period was greater than 6 hours or in persons dying of a chronic lingering disease. Adelson and colleagues commented that although the technique was simple, inexpensive, and used apparatus which was readily available, the standard error in cases of acute trauma dying within 6 hours was ± 5.75 hours for a PMI of 25 hours, but when all cases were included, the error was ± 10 hours (PMI not stated) which they considered too great to be of practical use in determining the PMI.

Sturner (1963) studied potassium concentration in the vitreous humor of 125 postmortem cases from both hospital and coroner's sources. Cases were excluded if the time of death was not accurately known, when the fluid was colored, cloudy, or contained particulate matter, when less than 0.5 mL was aspirated, and when the specimens were removed too long after autopsy. This left 69 analyses, both eyes being aspirated in 15 cases. The PMI varied widely from 3 to 104 hours. Sturner confirmed the arithmetic linear relationship between potassium concentration and the PMI up to 100 hours after death and he calculated a formula for the estimation of the PMI:

$$\text{PMI (in hours)} = (7.14 \times K^+ \text{concentration}) - 39.1 \qquad (3.1)$$

The error rate was ± 4.7 hours which did not increase with time, making it useful for determining the PMI after 24 hours. Sturner and Gantner (1964) expanded on this series of cases, examining the vitreous humor in 125 cadavers but they excluded cases where the time of death was not known to within 15 minutes, where the vitreous fluid was cloudy, colored, or contained particulate matter, where the amount of fluid aspirated was less than 0.5 mL, where the specimens were removed more than 24 hours after autopsy, and where technical problems arose. Sturner and Gantner distinguished coroners' cases from hospital cases and confirmed Sturner's previously quoted formula for estimating the PMI (Sturner, 1963). They confirmed that the potassium concentration in the coroners' cases increased in a linear, arithmetic manner with time up to 100 hours after death and it was not affected by temperature. The standard error of ± 4.7 up to 100 hours post mortem did not increase with time, and Adelson and colleagues' (1963) finding that the vitreous potassium concentration was much more variable in deaths in hospital patients compared with deaths from trauma, was confirmed with a standard error twice that of coroners' cases. They attributed this to an increase in serum potassium prior to death, to enzymatic influence, and to physiologic variation. Sturner and Gantner stated that the period from 24 hours after death and up to 100 hours represented the most useful working time of the procedure.

Sturner and Gantner also stated that it was generally accepted that vitreous potassium levels were dependent on and very nearly equal to the potassium content of serum but this could not be justified by the two studies referred to (Duke-Elder, 1929; Reddy and Kinsey, 1960). The first of these studies by Duke-Elder (1929) was carried out on the enucleated eyes of freshly slaughtered horses from an abattoir. The second study by Reddy and Kinsey (1960) analyzed the chemical content of the vitreous humor, aqueous humor, and plasma in living and then freshly killed rabbits. The potassium concentrations of the vitreous humor, the aqueous humor, and the plasma in Duke-Elder's study were found to be almost equal and it was postulated that the vitreous and aqueous humor were dialysates of capillary blood. Reddy and Kinsey could not explain the source, function, and distribution of the high potassium content of the vitreous fluid compared to that of the aqueous humor and plasma but postulated that there might be a positive and negative concentration gradient between posterior chamber aqueous and the vitreous humor. Henry and Smith (1980) stated in a review of the estimation of the PMI by chemical means that virtually no information was available about the antemortem composition of human intraocular fluids and this remains true at the present time (Madea and Musshoff, 2007).

Hughes (1965) reported contrary findings in a study of 117 cases of sudden death, both coroners' cases and hospital deaths, with PMIs up to 120 hours after death. The potassium concentration in each eye of every case was within 0.1 mEq/L. Hughes confirmed the increase in potassium concentration with increasing PMI, but found no consistent linear relationship between vitreous potassium concentration and the PMI, either with sudden deaths or with lingering hospital deaths and the time of death could not be put more accurately than within 24 hours. She concluded that measuring postmortem vitreous potassium concentration was an insufficient method for determining the PMI. Hansson and colleagues (1966) studied 203 autopsies in which the time of death was known to within 1 hour. Commenting that previous studies had only studied potassium concentrations up to about 40 hours, the present study was designed to determine whether estimation of the vitreous potassium was useful when the PMI was longer. There were two groups; one with an agonal period less than 6 hours and one with an agonal period longer than 6 hours and both groups included cases dying of accidental death and disease. The PMI varied from 3 to 310 hours. In 180 cases with a PMI up to 120 hours, a rising potassium concentration was observed after which time it remained constant. The potassium concentration did not differ according to the type of death or the agonal period. The standard error in the PMI determination was ± 20 hours up to 120 hours, twice as great as that reported by Adelson et al. (1963), after which it became even greater. Hansson and colleagues commented that the large error may have been due to technical difficulties in gathering and analyzing the specimens but, despite the results, the method might be of some use in cases where the secondary signs of death provided no help in determining the time of death. Lie's (1967) study of 88 hospital cases dying of various diseases, with a known time of death and a PMI varying from 2 to 95 hours, found a much smaller standard error of ± 4.7 hours for the PMI with a correlation coefficient of 0.99 using the formula suggested by Sturner (1963; see Eq. (3.1)). The arithmetic linear increase in potassium concentration with lengthening PMI was confirmed. Lie emphasized that all samples should be collected in a standard way in order to avoid any technical errors. There was no difference in potassium concentration between both eyes of the same cadaver and potassium concentrations did not differ significantly between fresh and refrigerated specimens of vitreous humor.

Leahy and Farber (1967) studied the postmortem chemistry of vitreous humor in a series of 52 cases. They estimated antemortem concentrations of sodium, chloride, and potassium as well as glucose and several enzymes, in blood collected within 24 hours of death and compared these concentrations with postmortem vitreous concentrations of the same substances. They found that vitreous potassium concentration rose erratically after death and it was not possible to calculate a normal postmortem range of any significance. Any mathematical relationship between vitreous potassium concentration and the PMI in 12 patients who had died suddenly was not apparent. They concluded that concentrations of sodium, chloride, and potassium in postmortem vitreous humor did not have evident clinicopathological correlation and, in particular, the unpredictable nature of postmortem potassium concentrations in determining the PMI did not justify its use. Coe (1969) studied 20 cases in which he analyzed postmortem vitreous electrolytes, including potassium, glucose, and other substances, in order to establish normal ranges for these substances and to determine which variations in these values reflected antemortem abnormalities and which reflected postmortem changes. The concentrations of these substances were compared with concentrations of the same substances in blood obtained from the heart. Coe found that the potassium concentration increased linearly for at least 100 hours after death, more rapidly within the first few hours but the rate of rise had marked individual variation. Because of this inconstant postmortem change the antemortem value of vitreous potassium would not be possible to be obtained by regression analysis. He agreed with Adelson et al. (1963), Hughes (1965), and Hansson et al. (1966) that although the potassium concentration rose arithmetically after death, there was such an individual variation in the rate of rise, especially after the first 24 hours, that it was of very limited value in determining the PMI. Coe (1969) found a standard error rate of ± 12 hours in the first 24 hours, growing increasingly larger after that time.

Adjutantis and Coutselinis (1972) proposed a method of estimating the PMI within the first 12 hours by estimating the vitreous potassium concentration and using the linear increase with time to extrapolate backwards in order to estimate the potassium concentration in life. They sampled 1 mL of vitreous humor from one eye after delivery of the body and then the same amount from the other eye, in the majority of cases at a 3-hour interval afterwards. Most cases died a violent death but the number of cases was not specified. The vitreous fluid was centrifuged and the potassium concentration determined by flame photometry. In a small number of cases, samples were taken from both eyes at the same time and the authors found that whatever variation of removal was used, there was no statistical difference in potassium concentration between the eyes. A statistical graph of potassium concentration plotted against time after death found a linear rise in potassium concentration up to 12 hours post mortem, after which time it ceased to increase. This was attributed to cessation of diffusion of potassium from autolyzing cells in the retina. Extrapolation of the regression slope, indicating potassium concentrations, backwards to its intersection with the axis denoting the PMI, indicated that the potassium concentration at the moment of death was 3.4 mEq/L. Adjutantis and Coutselinis calculated that in two-thirds of cases, the PMI could be estimated with an error rate of ± 1.1 hours within the first 12 hours. Henry and Smith (1980), however, commented that others had found the technique used by Adjutantis and Coutselinis unusable or that the error rate of the PMI was much greater, in the range of $\pm 10-26$ hours at 12 hours.

Balasooriya and colleagues (1984a) contradicted the findings of Adelson et al. (1963) who had found no bias in potassium concentrations from right and left eyes. Cases in which the PMI could be verified to within 15 minutes were studied and it was found that the potassium concentration in the vitreous humor varied between each eye, with a gradual linear increase in potassium concentration during the first 85 hours after death. When the potassium concentration was compared between the two eyes, 18.6% of the results varied by more than 10% from the mean of the two values, 50.8% were greater than 4% from the mean, and only 6 cases out of 59 had the same potassium concentrations in each eye. The differences were not related to the TSD or the mode of death but only a small quantity of 1 mL of fluid was withdrawn from each eye. Balasooriya and colleagues concluded that there were previously unreported differences in potassium concentration between the two eyes of any cadaver and this made it an unreliable estimate of the PMI.

Madea and colleagues (1989) commented that the estimation of vitreous potassium was not used in Germany to determine the PMI because the error rate varied so greatly between studies that it was not possible to determine which values to use. The various studies to that time averaged error rates between ± 9.5 and up to ± 40 hours in the first 100 hours after death and between ± 6 and ± 12 hours in the first 24 hours. The potassium concentration calculated in various studies also varied between 5 and 8 mEq/L and the rise in potassium concentration each hour after death varied between 0.1 and 0.2 mEq/L. Madea and colleagues postulated that electrolyte imbalances at the moment of death might be responsible for such large errors but studies on this aspect were lacking. They therefore studied 170 consecutive cases with an accurately known time of death comprised of 100 cases of sudden death and 70 cases of death following chronic disease.

The vitreous humor from both eyes was evacuated completely at the same time, centrifuged and analyzed measuring potassium, sodium, chloride, urea, and calcium concentrations. They found a 10% deviation from the mean potassium concentration in the vitreous humor of both eyes, which was independent of the TSD or mode of death. In this respect they agreed with Balasooriya et al.'s (1984a) findings. They therefore took the mean value of potassium concentration in both eyes in their study, in an attempt to narrow down or eliminate the wide range of error apparent from different studies. They again confirmed the linear relationship between vitreous potassium concentration and TSD, potassium concentrations steadily rising up to 120 hours post mortem. However, the error rate was ± 34 hours up to a PMI of 120 hours for all cases. To eliminate electrolyte imbalance at death as a cause for the error rate, cases with a urea concentration over 100 mg/dL (35.7 mmol/L) were removed from the study, as all these cases suffered from chronic disease before death. Madea and colleagues considered that the urea concentration was normally stable in postmortem vitreous humor and raised levels were most likely a marker of antemortem electrolyte imbalance. All cases with a urea concentration over 100 mg/dL (35.7 mmol/L) suffered from chronic disease. This reduced the number of cases to 138 and also reduced the error rate to a statistically significant ± 22 hours. Madea and colleagues thus eliminated most of the cases with chronic disease in which Adelson et al. (1963) had noted a greater range of scatter of the potassium concentration. To reduce the error rate further, they eliminated cases with an agonal period greater than 6 hours; a group in which Adelson et al. (1963) had also noted that there was a greater range of scatter of potassium concentration. The number of cases was reduced to 107 and the error rate to ± 20 hours, which, although within the 95% limits of confidence of the regression line, was not statistically significant. They concluded that other factors such as ambient temperature and blood alcohol level at the time of death could be possible factors in producing such a great error rate but that estimation of vitreous humor urea nitrogen concentration was a suitable standard to determine disturbed body metabolism before death. However, further studies were required to determine whether the arbitrarily chosen urea concentration of 100 mg/dL (35.7 mmol/L) should be reduced further in order to reduce the error rate. A major problem however was that normal antemortem values of vitreous potassium were unknown.

Madea and colleagues (1990) studied the potassium concentration in the vitreous humor of 100 cases of sudden natural or traumatic death, with a terminal period less than 6 hours and where the ambient temperature was below 50°F (10°C). The purpose of the study was to compare their formula for estimating the PMI from the vitreous potassium concentration with that of Sturner's (1963) formula (see (Eq. 3.1)). They found that the linear rate of increase of vitreous potassium concentration was faster than that found previously by Sturner, meaning that Sturner's model overestimated the PMI. In comparing their formula:

$$PMI = 5.26 \times K^+ \text{concentration} - 30.9, \tag{3.2}$$

with Sturner's formula (Eq. (3.1)), Madea and colleagues found a mean difference between real and extrapolated TSD of 15 hours up to 100 hours with Sturner's formula, compared with -0.26 hours using their formula. When they included the 138 cases in their previous study with a PMI over 30 hours and with urea values below 100 mg/dL (Madea et al., 1989), the mean difference rose to 26 hours with an error range of ± 41 hours at the 95% limits of confidence using Sturner's formula. Madea and colleagues concluded that the error of estimation of PMI was much less using their formula, but the error range within the 95% limits of confidence was still ± 20 hours up to 100 hours post mortem. Stephens and Richards (1987) studied postmortem vitreous potassium concentrations by withdrawing samples at known times after death and comparing them with the PMI. They analyzed 1427 samples from an unstated number of cases up to 35 hours post mortem and found a wide range of potassium concentrations for a known range of PMIs. For the first time in a study, vitreous potassium concentration was correlated with PMI as the dependent variable rather than the PMI being correlated with vitreous potassium concentration as the dependent variable. Very large or small potassium concentrations, which were attributed to abnormal deaths, were excluded. Stephens and Richards confirmed that the potassium concentration rose in a linear fashion but found that only 37.4% of potassium concentration variation was directly attributable to the PMI, the margin of error being ± 20 hours up to 35 hours post mortem. The other 62.6% of the variation in potassium concentration was unaccounted for, but might be due to factors such as variable ambient temperature, sampling technique, sex, age, ancestry, cause of death, or other unknown factors. Stephens and Richards suggested that studies focusing on the use of other chemical determinants in conjunction with potassium might prove useful.

ACCEPTANCE OF THE RELATIONSHIP OF VITREOUS POTASSIUM WITH THE PMI

Coe (1989) summed up progress regarding the estimation of the PMI from the vitreous potassium concentration in stating that there was no doubt there was a linear relationship between potassium concentration and the PMI, but whether it was a straight line or a biphasic one remained debatable. There was great variation in the error of estimation of the PMI between investigators, most reporting a standard error ranging from ± 4.7 to as high as ± 26 hours which increased as the PMI increased. There was also a large variation in the rate of increase of potassium concentration, from 0.14 mEq/L per hour found by Sturner (Sturner and Gantner, 1964; Sturner, 1963) to 0.55 mEq/L per hour determined by Adjutantis and Coutselinis (1972), with most values being about 0.17 mEq/L per hour. Coe suggested that these variations were due to both external and internal factors. The external factors were the sampling technique, the analytical instruments, the environmental temperature during the PMI and, most importantly, the temperature of the body during the PMI. The internal factors were the age of the individual, the duration of the terminal episode, and the presence or absence of nitrogen retention. Coe stated that the test was useful as long as these factors were properly evaluated in each individual case, and that he had found it to be of greatest value when the body had lain in a cool environment for several days and factors such as livor mortis, rigor mortis, and body temperature were in conflict or not able to be defined.

A different approach was adopted by Lange and colleagues (1994) when they analyzed 790 cases from six different studies carried out between 1963 and 1989. All studies graphed the rise in vitreous potassium concentration against the PMI. The relationship between the rise in potassium concentration and the PMI was not completely linear and the residual variability of the potassium concentration as a function of the PMI was not constant. All studies varied in the rate of rise in potassium concentration, that is, the slope of the regression line and in the intercept of the regression line on the y-axis, indicating that the theoretical potassium concentration at the time of death varied between studies. In general, the authors suggested that determination of the PMI from measured vitreous potassium concentration was best done when the PMI was no later than 24 hours, but rough estimates could extend to 48–72 hours, especially in cold environments. Lange and colleagues suggested that the large error rate in estimating the PMI was due to several factors. Firstly, all the studies assumed that the relationship between vitreous potassium concentration and the PMI was linear but Lange and colleagues found that even after statistically transforming the data it was not linear, due to the inability to adjust for factors across all studies, such as age, mode of death, and sampling technique. Secondly, the confidence limits had been incorrectly defined as the confidence limits for the estimated slope of the line indicating increasing potassium concentration instead of for the estimated value of the PMI. Thirdly, the inverse prediction method of Stephens and Richards (1987), the only other study to have used the method, was more correct, that is, where the PMI depended on the vitreous potassium concentration rather than vitreous potassium concentration depending on the PMI. Because of the nonlinearity of the regression line in the studies examined, Lange and colleagues statistically constructed a nonlinear, smooth, loess curve and fitted the confidence limits to this. This produced a much reduced margin of error. For potassium concentrations less than 7 mEq/L the error range of the PMI up to 10 hours was ± 1 hour. For potassium concentrations between 7 and 12 mEq/L it was ± 2 hours and for concentrations between 12 and 18 mEq/L it was ± 3 hours for a PMI between 36 and 80 hours and for concentrations greater than 18 mEq/L it was ± 5 hours and increasing. As the potassium concentration increased above this level, the error in the PMI greatly increased and the estimation of the PMI became unreliable. Commenting on Lange and colleagues' study in his review, Madea (2005) stated that if these error limits were accurate, it would be almost the perfect method but he was unable to verify the accuracy after testing it on his own forensic cases.

A study was carried out by Muñoz et al. (2001) using the inverse prediction method of Stephens and Richards (1987) in order to construct a new formula using vitreous potassium concentration to estimate the PMI. They studied 201 samples of vitreous humor, withdrawing all the fluid from both eyes from 164 bodies in which the time of death could be verified to within 15 minutes. Opaque specimens of vitreous and those from infants less than 6 months old were discarded. The minimum PMI was 1 hour and the maximum was 40.45 hours with an average of 11 hours and samples from corpses where the TSD could not be established to within ± 15 minutes were excluded. There were no significant differences in potassium concentration between both eyes and all samples were classified into two groups; one group had no known metabolic disturbance, usually those where a sudden natural or traumatic death had occurred while the second group had a metabolic disturbance before death such as in a chronic illness. The authors compared the two methods of estimating the PMI, that is, when the PMI was dependent on the potassium concentration and when the potassium concentration was dependent on the PMI. They found a greater error rate when the PMI was the independent variable and the vitreous potassium concentration was the dependent variable than when the vitreous potassium concentration was the independent variable and the PMI was the dependent variable. Muñoz and colleagues calculated a formula which explained 70.1% of the variation in the data, compared with 57.5% explained with the other more traditional method. Removing cases with a urea concentration >30 mg/dL and a creatinine concentration ≥ 0.5 mg/dL further reduced the error rate. They suggested that the remaining error was possibly caused by race, age, sampling technique, and general lack of standardization.

RECENT ADVANCES AND THE CURRENT STATUS OF RESEARCH INTO VITREOUS POTASSIUM

In a wide-ranging review of postmortem chemistry research, Coe (1993) stated that routine examinations of vitreous electrolytes, glucose, and urea nitrogen alone would provide information in determining the cause of death or time of death in up to 5% of all forensic cases and proper analysis of blood, CSF, vitreous humor, pericardial fluid, and other body fluids would help in about 10% of cases. Coe reviewed the postmortem analysis of carbohydrates, nitrogen compounds, electrolytes, lipids, proteins and immunological proteins, bile pigments, enzymes, and hormones. He concluded that the postmortem fall in glucose concentrations in vitreous humor was too erratic to be of use in estimating PMI, and that measuring concentrations of lactic, ascorbic, and pyruvic acids, and inositol was not useful. He commented that at various times, measurements of serum non-protein nitrogen, vitreous ammonia, CSF amino acids, vitreous creatine and hypoxanthine, vitreous and CSF potassium, vitreous calcium and blood pH, had all been proposed for use in the estimation of the PMI, but that most had only been investigated by a single source and there had been no follow-up studies or independent verification. The exception was the measurement of vitreous potassium concentrations which had been studied extensively. Coe concluded that this seemed to be the best biochemical test available for the estimation of PMIs longer than 24 hours, but in the first 24 hours the margin of error was too great for it to be useful.

Tagliaro and colleagues (1998) published a paper explaining capillary zone electrophoresis. Capillary electrophoresis, first reported by Hjertén (1967), was a system of dispersion of fluid through narrow-bore tubes made of chemically and electrically inert materials. A second study by Tagliaro and colleagues (1999) investigated the estimation of vitreous potassium concentration by capillary zone electrophoresis in order to try to eliminate the differences between the various methods of collection and analysis of vitreous potassium concentration, which had made the comparison of different studies difficult. Each element had different speeds of migration dispersion when an electrical current was applied to the tubing and the dispersions could be measured. In the early 1990s advances had made it possible to carry out more rapid analysis of ions. Only a very small quantity of vitreous humor was required for analysis. It was injected through a buffer solution of imidazole, 18-crown-6 ether, and α-hydroxybutyric acid, buffered to a pH of 4.5 and then passed through a very fine silica capillary tube with a transparent window. By running an electric current between buffer solutions, an electric field was produced as the vitreous humor passed along the capillary tubing, causing the various ions to move at different rates according to their electrical charge. Thus the concentration of each ion could be measured using ultraviolet absorption detection. The study compared the analysis of potassium concentration in the vitreous humor of 12 real autopsy specimens by capillary electrophoresis with analysis by flame photometry. The results were well correlated ($r^2 = 0.9333$). It was also possible to analyze other ions within the vitreous humor, including ammonia, calcium, and sodium. Tagliaro and colleagues then tested the potassium concentrations in 20 cadavers with a PMI varying between 5 and 96 hours and also found a high correlation ($r^2 = 0.904$) between potassium concentrations and the PMI. They concluded that electrophoresis was a simple, accurate method requiring a minimal amount of fluid and it was suitable for forensic application.

A study by Ferslew and colleagues (1998) also found a high correlation ($r = 0.9642$) between the potassium concentrations in the vitreous humor of 25 forensic autopsy specimens when analyzed by both capillary electrophoresis and by flame photometry. They concluded that electrophoresis offered an accurate and more automated method of potassium analysis than flame photometry. A further study by Tagliaro and colleagues (2001) tested the correlation of potassium concentrations in both eyes in 57 cases of natural or violent death using capillary electrophoresis, in which the PMI was known exactly. The PMI varied from 7 to 144 hours and they found a highly significant linear correlation between potassium concentration and the PMI ($r = 0.89$, $p < 0.0001$). In addition, there was no statistically significant difference in potassium concentration between the two eyes of a body at the same PMI. This finding was different from other studies which did find significant differences in potassium concentration between the two eyes from the same cadaver (Balasooriya et al., 1984a; Madea et al., 1990; Pounder et al., 1998). Tagliaro and colleagues suggested that their anomalous finding was due to only removing a small quantity of vitreous humor (50 μL). The other studies had removed much larger quantities of vitreous humor which might have reduced pressure on the cells of the eye tissues, leading to an artificially high release of potassium.

In order to try to improve the statistical correlation between PMI and potassium concentration in vitreous humor, Bocaz-Beneventi and colleagues (2002) estimated the concentrations of sodium, potassium, and ammonium in the vitreous humor of 61 cadavers by capillary zone electrophoresis after diluting the vitreous in an aqueous solution of barium. The PMI was known in each case, the intervals varying from 3 hours up to 87 hours with only three cases being over 100 hours. The average PMI, discounting the three cases over 100 hours, was 41 hours. Only 50 μL of vitreous fluid was removed from each eye. They analyzed the results by using the chemical estimations as input data and the PMIs as output data in a computer-generated program (Neural Network Stimulator, release 3.0D, TRAJAN software, 1998). Using this method they were able to reduce the error in estimating the PMI from approximately ± 15.28 hours using potassium estimation by single-ion analysis and linear least squares regression to 4.69 hours using the computer software program.

In a critical review of methods of estimating the PMI by biochemical methods, Madea (2005) stated that all chemical methods of determining the TSD up to the time of writing were of very limited value in practice, since they were neither precise nor reliable and did not give an immediate result at the scene of a crime, but he also observed that some progress had been made in methodology. Most chemical methods measured concentration changes in different fluid compartments, which were caused by metabolic and autolytic changes influenced by temperature, disease, cause of death, length of the terminal phase before death, and the site and method of sample acquisition. Because of these factors, variation between individuals was so great that chemical methods were of little use in practice.

Although the postmortem measurement of vitreous humor potassium concentration had been extensively studied and was widely used, Madea (2005) listed the deficiencies with its use, namely:

1. A number of linear regression equations comparing the potassium concentration with environmental temperature had been produced with varying gradients of the regression line, indicating that analysis was not standardized.
2. The state of health and chronic illness of an individual might influence the potassium concentration. By eliminating cases with a vitreous urea concentration >100 mg/dL and a terminal episode greater than 6 hours, the PMI could be reduced from ± 34 hours, but only to ± 22 and ± 20 hours, respectively, over a PMI of up to 130 hours.
3. By using potassium concentration as the independent variable and the PMI as the dependent variable instead of the reverse, the accuracy of estimating the PMI was increased from ± 25.96 to ± 23.27 hours over a PMI up to 130 hours, but this improvement was not statistically significant.
4. The reported increased accuracy of estimating the PMI by using a loess curve, as reported by Lange et al. (1994), revealed very high false estimations of the PMI when independently tested. The reliability of this method of statistical evaluation therefore remained unclear.

Madea (2005) further commented that by using multiple linear regression analysis of sodium, glucose, and urea as well as potassium, the error rate in estimation of the PMI was reduced from ± 16.2 to ± 14 hours and using capillary zone electrophoresis as a method of determining all ions was promising, reducing the estimation of PMI to an error rate of ± 3 hours compared to ± 15 hours over a PMI of up to 200 hours when potassium alone was used. However this method had only been used in a small study group of 61 cases (Bocaz-Beneventi et al., 2002). The variation in vitreous humor potassium concentrations was not only due to instrumentation, but also the composition of vitreous humor itself and the preanalytical handling. Development of a calibrated method for analysis would be one of the tasks for the future.

A further review of a sample of 492 cases consisting of 170 of their own cases analyzing vitreous potassium, 176 cases from Muñoz et al. (2001) analyzing vitreous potassium, and 198 cases in which vitreous hypoxanthine was analyzed, was carried out by Madea and Rödig (2006). The aims of the study were firstly to examine the finding by Muñoz and colleagues that more accuracy was gained in estimating the time of death by using potassium concentration as the independent variable and the PMI as the dependent variable and secondly to examine if in fact greater accuracy in estimating the PMI was possible by using the loess curve as proposed by Lange et al. (1994). Madea and Rödig estimated the PMI up to 133 hours and confirmed a greater, but only marginally better accuracy, from ± 25.96 to ± 23.27 hours, in estimating the PMI when potassium concentration was used as the independent variable and the PMI as the dependent variable. Madea and Rödig's evaluation of estimating the PMI by using the loess curve, as recommended by Lange et al. (1994), revealed a systematic overestimation of the TSD, suggesting the use of a loess curve to estimate the PMI could not be sustained.

Finally, an important review by Madea and Musshoff (2007) outlined the difficulties and inaccuracies in the use of vitreous humor potassium concentration analysis. The chemical analysis of vitreous fluid differed from that of the analysis of blood, serum, or urine in that standard procedures of analysis and calibration in these latter fluids had been readily attained in life and could therefore be compared in postmortem samples. However, the normal value in life of vitreous potassium concentration could not be determined and if, and how fast, abnormal serum potassium concentrations equilibrated with vitreous potassium concentrations in life could not be ascertained. It was also not known if potassium concentration was stable in postmortem vitreous humor. In all studies to that date, correlations between antemortem serum and postmortem vitreous values were completely absent. The concentrations of vitreous potassium determined by ion-specific electrodes tended to be higher than those determined by flame photometry. For all these reasons, the term "normal vitreous value" was a misnomer and instead the term "reference value" should be used. Madea and Musshoff defined reference values as a set of values of a certain type of quantity available from a single individual or group of individuals corresponding to a stated description which must be defined and available if others were to use the reference values. They further defined reference individuals as comprising a reference population from which was selected a reference sample group on which were determined reference values and on which was observed a reference distribution from which were calculated reference limits that might define reference intervals. The reference values should be specifically stated for the reference population, as well as the environmental and physical conditions, specimen collection, transport, preparation, storage, and analytical method used. No study in the literature on reference values to that date fulfilled all these requirements.

Another problem with the use of vitreous potassium analysis was that of the development of a calibrated and validated method for vitreous humor potassium analysis. Most instruments used were calibrated for serum but it was questionable whether these instruments could be used for vitreous analysis as well. Methods of preanalytical collection and handling also required to be standardized. Developing a calibrated and validated method for vitreous humor analysis would be one of the tasks for the future.

THE ESTIMATION OF HYPOXANTHINE IN VITREOUS HUMOR

Another method of analyzing vitreous humor as a means of determining the PMI was investigated by Rognum and colleagues (1991), who studied the levels of hypoxanthine in vitreous humor. Hypoxanthine (6-hydroxypurine) is a naturally occurring purine derivative and a deaminated form of adenine, itself a breakdown product of adenosine monophosphate (AMP). Hypoxanthine exists as an intermediate in the biodegradation of AMP. AMP is converted to xanthine and then uric acid by the enzyme xanthine oxidase before it is excreted as urate (Harkness, 1988). Increased levels of hypoxanthine in the plasma of the umbilical cord of newborn infants suffering from intrauterine hypoxia compared with the umbilical cord plasma levels of hypoxanthine from normal newborn infants had first been reported by Saugstad (1975), who attributed the increased levels to hypoxia which caused an increase in AMP break down and consequently an increase in hypoxanthine concentration. The hypoxanthine concentration was also thought to increase due to decreased transformation of hypoxanthine to uric acid by the inhibition of the enzyme xanthine oxidase. Saugstad and Olaisen (1978) investigated hypoxanthine levels in the vitreous humor of 86 individuals between 0.5 and 192 hours after death to determine whether these levels reflected the degree of tissue hypoxia preceding death. Cases were divided into five groups depending on the cause of death; severe trauma causing death, cases of strangulation or suspension, death from myocardial infarction, fatal drug intoxication, and the last group included cases of bronchopneumonia, gastric hemorrhage, brain catastrophes, drowning, and carbon monoxide poisoning. There was no statistical difference in hypoxanthine concentration in any of the groups except in the group dying of fatal intoxication, in which the concentration was significantly increased. As the normal concentration of hypoxanthine in the vitreous humor in life was not known, the authors considered the values in cases of sudden death to reflect the concentration during life. They therefore took the mean concentration found in cases dying from severe trauma and myocardial infarction as reflecting the normal concentration before death and considered this concentration as the reference value. It was between 0 and 540 μmol/L and was 10−20 times higher than the plasma concentration. Although in the cases used for the reference values (trauma and myocardial infarction) there was no significant difference in hypoxanthine concentration in samples obtained more than 48 hours post mortem compared with samples obtained between 0 and 48 hours; in the total samples from all groups tested, a positive correlation was found between hypoxanthine concentration and the PMI, the concentration rising in a linear manner with the passage of time when it exceeded 48 hours. Compared with the reference group there was no increased concentration of hypoxanthine in cases dying with tissue hypoxia such as suspension or strangulation, presumably because the period of hypoxia was short but there was a significant elevation in cases dying of drug intoxication, which Saugstad and Olaisen attributed to prolonged tissue hypoxia before death. They concluded that the hypoxanthine concentration in the vitreous humor post mortem might give information about whether or not tissue hypoxia preceded circulatory arrest.

The next important study was by Rognum and colleagues (1991) who studied the influence of postmortem time and temperature on the hypoxanthine concentration in vitreous humor and compared it to the potassium concentration in order to determine if this chemical substance was less prone to error than the potassium concentration estimation. In most cases four samples of vitreous humor, twice from each eye, were taken from 87 subjects within 120 hours after death. The exact time of death was known in all cases. Causes of death varied, but were mainly from myocardial infarctions and accidents. The bodies were kept at various temperatures: 5°C (33 subjects), 10°C (16 subjects), 15°C (16 subjects), and 23°C (23 subjects). Hypoxanthine concentration was determined by liquid chromatography and potassium by flame photometry. The results were graphed with chemical concentrations on the x-axis and PMI in hours on the y-axis. In 19 subjects in which the vitreous was extracted within 1.5 hours of death, regression analyses were performed to determine the intercept and therefore the normal levels at the time of death. These values were estimated at 5.8 mmol/L for potassium and 7.6 μmol/L for hypoxanthine. It was found that in all subjects the increase in hypoxanthine and potassium concentrations correlated with time, but only after 48 hours post mortem and that the longer the time interval after death, up to 192 hours, the greater the correlation. The higher the ambient temperature, the greater were the hypoxanthine and the potassium concentrations at a similar time, that is, the steeper were the slopes of the regression lines. For the group as a whole the potassium and hypoxanthine concentrations were significantly correlated ($r = 0.93$, $p < 0.001$). During the first hours after death the scatter of concentration values about the regression line was less with hypoxanthine than with potassium which the authors suggested might be due to the influence of raised urea and possibly alcohol levels affecting the vitreous potassium concentration. Hypoxanthine concentration in vitreous humor had been previously shown to be influenced by ante-mortem hypoxia (Madea et al., 1994; Saugstad, 1975) and the authors suggested that this might also be the case with potassium. Therefore the method should only be used in estimating the PMI in cases of sudden death without antemortem hypoxia. Rognum and colleagues stressed that this was only a preliminary study on a small number of cases and that further studies were desirable to determine whether the estimation of hypoxanthine in the vitreous humor was useful in estimating the PMI.

A different finding was made by Madea and colleagues (1994) when they studied postmortem hypoxanthine and potassium concentrations in the vitreous humor of 92 bodies with a known TSD, in order to evaluate statistical parameters for determining more precisely, the PMI estimation for vitreous hypoxanthine in comparison to vitreous potassium. The vitreous humor was completely removed from each eye at the same time. In an additional 43 bodies, vitreous humor was removed from both eyes at timed intervals between 2 and 20 hours. These cases had all died either from sudden natural causes or trauma with brief terminal episodes. Analysis was carried out by the same methods that Rognum and colleagues (1991) had used. It was confirmed that the hypoxanthine concentration rose in a linear fashion as the PMI increased, the rise beginning immediately post mortem, in contrast to the findings of Saugstad and Olaisen (1978) who noted an interval of 48−72 hours before the concentration rose. The potassium concentration also rose, but the potassium concentration had a much stronger correlation with the PMI than the hypoxanthine concentration ($r = 0.925$ for potassium compared with $r = 0.714$ for hypoxanthine). The 95% confidence limits were ± 17 hours for potassium and ± 32 hours for hypoxanthine up to 120 hours post mortem. The greater scatter of potassium concentration levels compared with those of hypoxanthine was not confirmed by this study. In the cases of timed bilateral withdrawal of vitreous humor, there were greater inter-individual differences between the rises in the concentration of hypoxanthine than with potassium. In commenting on the differences in findings between their study and that of Rognum et al. (1991), Madea and colleagues suggested that one reason might be the repeated taking of small samples, which disturbed the concentration gradient between the retinal cells and the center of the globe, giving a false value when considering the total concentration: a true value could only be obtained by sampling the whole vitreous humor. A second reason might be the fact that hypoxanthine increased in postmortem vitreous due to irreversible circulatory arrest, anoxemia, and diffusion, but that during vital hypoxia there was an accelerated catabolism of AMP to hypoxanthine which accumulated in body tissues and fluids. A final reason could be due to the differing metabolism of potassium and hypoxanthine at death. Potassium had different concentrations in different intra- and extracellular body compartments during life but with loss of selective membrane permeability at death it would diffuse along a concentration gradient, for example, in the globe of the eye from the retina into the center of the vitreous. Potassium concentration was regulated during life in narrow ranges. In contrast hypoxanthine, a degradation product of adenosine nucleotide degradation, was formed by several enzymatic reactions before diffusing along the concentration gradient from the retina into the center of the vitreous. Theoretically, therefore, a substance (potassium) whose post mortem increase was slow due to diffusion, would have a stronger correlation with the TSD than a substance (hypoxanthine) whose post mortem increase was due to degradation as well as diffusion. Madea and colleagues concluded that the rise in vitreous potassium concentration after death was a more reliable guide to PMI estimation than the vitreous hypoxanthine concentration which could be affected by antemortem hypoxia.

Finally, Madea (2005) commented that the stronger linear correlation of hypoxanthine concentrations compared with potassium concentrations, with the PMI, in vitreous humor, as claimed by Rognum et al. (1991) had not been sustained by further studies and that death time estimation was more precise using vitreous potassium concentration than using hypoxanthine concentration (Madea et al., 1994; Muñoz Barús et al., 2002). More recent studies have also confirmed this finding (Madea and Rödig, 2006; Abdel Salam et al., 2012).

CHEMICAL INVESTIGATION OF SYNOVIAL FLUID

Synovial fluid in a closed joint compartment would seem to offer an alternative site to vitreous humor for chemical analysis, but there have been few studies examining this fluid as an alternative to estimating the time of death. In one study by Madea and colleagues (2001) the concentrations of sodium, potassium, calcium, chloride, urea, creatinine, and glucose in the suprapatellar pouch synovial fluid were compared with the same concentrations in the vitreous humor of 74 cases of sudden death, with a PMI ranging from 6 to 126 hours, which had no joint disease (defined as "rheumatism" and "arthritis"), no metabolic disorders, and received no resuscitation with intravenous fluids prior to death. Only glucose and potassium were useful with regard to estimation of the PMI but the authors concluded that synovial fluid was a useful alternative fluid to estimate postmortem potassium concentration if the vitreous humor was not available. A second study by Sheikh (2007) of suprapatellar synovial fluid from 123 cadavers using potassium analysis by flame photometry in which the PMI was known, confirmed the linear relationship of potassium concentration with the PMI up to 48 hours after death. Sheikh concluded that it was a useful alternative to vitreous humor in the analysis of potassium although more difficult to handle and analyze because of the higher viscosity.

Tumram and colleagues (2011) analyzed both the synovial fluid and vitreous humor in 154 cases where the time of death was known, up to 35 hours post mortem. Cases of metabolic disease and injury to the knees were excluded and analysis of sodium, potassium, chloride, calcium, creatinine, glucose, and urea was carried out by capillary zone electrophoresis. There was no correlation between these chemical substances and the PMI except for potassium. The authors confirmed that potassium concentration rose in a linear fashion after death in both synovial fluid and vitreous humor but that the strength of the relationship between potassium concentration and PMI was greater with synovial fluid ($r = 0.7873$) than with vitreous humor ($r = 0.527$). Finally a study by Siddhamsetty and colleagues (2014), examining the synovial fluid from the suprapatellar pouch of 210 cases post mortem, confirmed the linear relationship between the rise in potassium concentration and the PMI in synovial fluid. Cases were separated into 12-hour periods of the time of death from 0 hours up to 72 hours after death. The authors found no relationship between PMI and sodium, chloride, calcium, and glucose concentrations. There was a positive correlation between increasing synovial fluid potassium concentration and the PMI up to 72 hours ($r = 0.840$).

BIOMARKERS OF THE PMI IN THE BONE MARROW AND OTHER BODY ORGANS

Porteous (1961) studied the viability of bone marrow cells in 50 cadavers at varying times after death in order to determine whether cadaver bone marrow could be used for transplanting. He found that motility in cells was maintained for 20 hours or more after death in refrigerated subjects, but the motility time was shortened if pyrexia had occurred before death. He did not, however, link this method to estimation of the PMI. In an attempt to establish a basis for correlating antemortem and postmortem bone marrow findings in patients with hematological disease, Hoffman and colleagues (1964) studied the bone marrow aspirated from 20 subjects, ranging from 30 minutes to 15 hours after death and who had died from a variety of diseases, and from trauma, in order to establish quantitative chronological trends in the counts of the various cell types. The authors found, in common with other investigators, that mature cellular types were usually indistinguishable 10–19 hours after death. They were unable to demonstrate a significant difference in the rate of cellular autolysis based on age, sex, or mode of death. Despite these findings, Hoffman and colleagues suggested that it was conceivable that the study of postmortem bone marrow could be perfected as an ancillary medicolegal method for establishing the time of death. Penttilä and Laiho (1981) examined the functionality and morphology of the different cellular components of blood in 123 cadavers kept at 4°C from 1.7 to 270.4 hours after death. They concluded that for a short period after death certain cellular properties could be applied to the postmortem diagnosis of diseases but were of minor use for the estimation of the TSD. Twenty years later a study by Dokgöz and colleagues (2001) on the morphology of white blood cells after death reached similar conclusions that the speed of the changes were so variable as to make it difficult to estimate the TSD. These were also the findings of Bardale and Dixit (2007). A second study by Penttilä and Laiho (1981) examined the viability of a number of blood and other organ cells after death in the same 123 cadavers used in their other study, after staining the cells with trypan blue in a buffer solution (Laiho and Penttilä, 1981). Cells from the spleen, lymph nodes, lung, and bone marrow as well as white blood cells and spermatozoa were examined. The loss of viability of white blood cells showed a moderate correlation with the postmortem period up to about 270 hours in cadavers kept at +4°C but the great variability between individual results made this an uncertain method of estimating the TSD.

Vass and colleagues (2002) studied the amino acids produced by autolysis of protein in the heart, kidneys, liver, brain, and muscle of 18 cadavers allowed to decompose naturally over a 4-year period in an attempt to identify biomarkers that might be useful in determining the PMI. The authors acknowledged that the most important variables affecting putrefaction were temperature and, to a lesser extent, humidity. The time of death, the air temperature record after death, and the cause of death were known and chemical analysis of the tissue from various organs was carried out at autopsy. The PMI was measured in cumulative degree hours, defined as the average temperature in degrees Centigrade cumulatively added for each 12-hour period. Although there was a large variability among subjects there were consistent patterns of biomarker relationships that appeared at different time intervals and which persisted across the entire set of subjects. Vass and colleagues used these patterns as the basis for determining the PMI, by producing flow charts which outlined the appearance of the various amino acids at specific time intervals after death. The disadvantage of this method was that it was organ-specific, a different pattern of amino acid concentration being applicable for different organs. However, if more organs were analyzed, the accuracy of PMI estimation was increased.

Two further studies which have not been followed by further research but which showed some promise in estimating the PMI are worthy of mention. The first by Gos and Raszeja (1993) examined the postmortem activity of the enzymes lactate (LDH) and malate dehydrogenase (MDH) in human liver. Twenty-five cadavers which had died from nontoxic causes were studied. Samples of liver were removed from the cadavers within 12 hours of death, each divided into five parts and stored at different temperatures and examined every day for 14 days then every 7 days for 35 days. The activity of LDH and MDH was examined in each sample and the authors found a good correlation between declining activity of both enzymes with increasing PMI when mathematically expressed by linear regression equations. Gos and Raszeja recommended further follow-up studies.

The second study by Myo Thaik-Oo and colleagues (2002) examined the concentration of vascular endothelial growth factor (VEGF), a glycoprotein with potent angiogenic, mitogenic, and vascular permeability-enhancing activities, in the brain, lungs, heart, liver, and kidneys from 19 cadavers in order to determine whether there was a correlation with the PMI. The PMI ranged from 1 to 120 hours and the authors found that the VEGF concentration increased linearly with the PMI up to 20 hours in the lungs and kidneys, up to 15 hours in the liver, and in the brain it started to increase after 24 hours, continued up to 40 hours after which time it began to fall. In the heart there was no clear correlation between the PMI and the VEGF level. Myo Thaik-Oo and colleagues concluded that the estimation of VEGF from certain organs might be useful in the estimation of the TSD in the early postmortem period but that additional studies were required.

IMMUNOHISTOCHEMISTRY

From 1999 to 2001 Wehner and colleagues published three papers describing the immunological detection of insulin from pancreatic β-cells (Wehner et al., 1999), thyroglobulin from thyroid follicular cells (Wehner et al., 2000), and calcitonin from the c-cells of the thyroid gland (Wehner et al., 2001). The authors used animal antibodies to detect the antigens insulin, thyroglobulin, and calcitonin in three similar studies, in which over 100 cadavers were included in each study. The time of death was known in every cadaver. The principle behind the study was that as the PMI increases the antigens, which are proteins, become denatured and can no longer be detected by staining methods. Detection was made up to 45 days post mortem with insulin and up to 21 days with thyroglobulin and calcitonin. Insulin was detected in all cases with a positive immunological reaction up to 12 days post mortem, an equivocal reaction between 13 and 29 days, and a negative reaction after 30 days. With thyroglobulin the figures were: all cases positive up to 5 days, equivocal between 6 and 12 days, and negative after 13 days. With calcitonin, all cases were positive up to 4 days, equivocal between 5 and 12 days, and negative after 13 days. The authors inferred from these studies that detection, or lack of detection, of these antigens may be of use in estimating the PMI within the stated time intervals.

Erlandsson and Munro (2007) investigated the PMI in beagle dogs. Ten dogs, grouped in pairs for similar weight and sex, were euthanased, kept in similar environmental conditions, and autopsied at intervals of 24, 48, and 72 hours, 7 days, and 23 days. Rectal temperatures were recorded as well as pathological and histological changes in the lungs, heart, liver, urinary bladder, thyroid, pancreas, and tonsils. Immunohistochemistry of the cervical and tracheal lymph nodes was carried out, specifically staining the B and T lymphocytes. The authors found that after 3 days and up to 23 days there was a gradual decrease in B lymphocyte staining as the PMI increased, whereas the T lymphocytes continued to stain strongly. It was suggested that further research might lead to immunological tools for the estimation of the time of death. Immunochemistry might therefore provide a method of estimating the TSD in the later stages of decomposition. Of interest also in this study was that over the first 10 hours post mortem, rectal temperature was useful in determining the PMI, within a range of ± 2 hours and the authors determined that it was possible to develop a table of histological changes in the heart, liver, lungs, pancreas, and tonsils that might indicate the TSD.

HIGH-RESOLUTION PROTON MAGNETIC RESONANCE SPECTROSCOPY

A study in 1988 showed that the quantitative estimation of brain metabolites by high-resolution proton nuclear magnetic resonance spectroscopy in rabbit brains might be useful to identify certain metabolic substances which became elevated in the postmortem period, while N-acetyl aspartate and the total creatine pool, which did not become elevated, might be used as reference matabolites (Petroff et al., 1988). Fineschi and colleagues (1990) confirmed the concept behind this principle in their study on rat skeletal muscle. They concluded that careful consideration of the relative peak intensities of all the detectable NMR resonances such as lactate, histidine, amino acids, and adenine nucleotide, was very likely to provide a good estimate of the postmortem time. Ith and colleagues (2002a) extended the study scanning eight sheep heads and four postmortem human heads to determine the nature and quantity of metabolites occurring up to 2−3 weeks' post mortem. After 3 days new metabolites, not present in life, and which included free trimethylammonium, propionate, butyrate, and iso-butyrate, began to appear and to increase in quantity. They concluded that further study of these metabolites might be of use as a means of quantitatively determining the PMI. In a further study of a number of metabolites in sheep and human brains by Ith and colleagues (2002b) it was found that changes in concentration detected by ^{1}H-MR spectroscopy varied with the passage of time. Increased concentration of some followed a sigmoid curve, others were unpredictable but those in which the increase in concentration followed a linear course such as propionate, alanine, acetate, and γ-amino butyric acid (GABA), could be useful in predicting the PMI up to 250 hours. The mathematical models derived from sheep were successfully applied in four human bodies but the authors concluded that further studies were required to determine the influence of temperature. This method remains in the experimental field at present but Madea (2005) in a review of biochemical methods of predicting the PMI commented that the method showed promise. The reasons were that it was a noninvasive method of quantitative measurement in which longitudinal studies with reproducible results were possible and that influencing factors such as temperature could be easily studied.

ELECTROLYTE CONCENTRATIONS IN CSF

There have been few studies on the chemical analysis of CSF and even less in conjunction with the estimation of the PMI. Mason et al. (1951) estimated the rise in potassium concentration in 46 cadavers from 1.5 to 70 hours after death in order to determine if there was a correlation with the PMI. They found that if potassium concentration was plotted against the logarithm of time, a fair approximation to a straight line was produced but the error was too great for the TSD to be estimated. Madea et al. (1994) found that both the potassium and the hypoxanthine concentrations in CSF were so confounding that neither could be recommended for practical use in the estimation of the TSD. Wyler et al. (1994) published a study in which they were able to correlate the increasing cell count in postmortem CSF with the PMI. They studied two groups of cadavers; 35 were maintained at 20°C, placed on their backs and lumbar punctures carried out at different intervals from 3 to 39 hours post mortem. A second group of 34 bodies were maintained at 4°C and lumbar punctures carried out at intervals from 3 to 53 hours post mortem. No cases with disease of the central nervous system were included and the time of death was known in all cases. In some cases CSF was obtained by cisternal puncture. Three groups of cells could be identified, lymphocytoid, monocytoid, and reticular cells, and the authors were able to compute mathematical models to estimate the TSD. They concluded that their first results suggested a correlation between the cell count in postmortem CSF and the PMI but further studies would be necessary to investigate the influence of temperature, body position, and to establish confidence intervals of the estimations.

Yadav and colleagues (2007) claimed to have found a significant correlation between sodium and potassium concentrations and the sodium/potassium ratio in CSF up to 25 hours after death. One hundred cadavers, in which the time of death was known, had CSF extracted from the lateral ventricles after opening the skull, whereas previous researchers had obtained CSF by cisternal puncture, a blind procedure, and one which risked contamination by blood products. Up to 25 hours after death, a postmortem increase in potassium concentration and decrease in sodium concentration was found. The rise in potassium concentration showed a statistically significant correlation with the PMI. The fall in sodium concentration also correlated significantly with the PMI as did the sodium and potassium ion ratio, but to a lesser extent. The cause of death or environmental temperature did not significantly alter the results. The researchers concluded that the ratio of sodium and potassium concentration was a better predictor of PMI than the estimation of either electrolyte concentration alone. However, the research depended on obtaining CSF from the lateral ventricles of the brain at autopsy, and Yadav and colleagues concluded that further studies were required to determine the PMI in cases where sodium and potassium concentrations were abnormal at the time of death.

There have been few studies using CSF components to estimate the TSD because cells lining the subarachnoid space in the brain autolyze rapidly and limit the use of CSF in analysis (Naumann, 1959).

ELECTROLYTE CONCENTRATIONS IN PERICARDIAL FLUID

Balasooriya and colleagues (1984b) examined concentrations of potassium, sodium, calcium, phosphate, alkaline phosphatase, alanine aminotransferase, gammaglutamyl transferase, hydroxybutyric dehydrogenase, glutamic oxaloacetic transaminase, creatine phosphokinase, bicarbonate, urea, creatinine, direct, indirect and total bilirubin, urate, iron, and cholesterol in the pericardial fluid obtained from 74 cadavers and in whom the time of death was known to within 15 minutes, in order to ascertain whether there was any correlation between the concentrations of these substances and the PMI. The authors instanced only one previous study of postmortem pericardial fluid in 1976 and published in German (Brinkman et al., 1976). Although they found an increase in the concentration of some of the electrolytes with increasing PMI the changes were not sufficiently constant or predictable to allow an accurate estimate of the PMI. Balasooriya and colleagues commented that analysis of vitreous humor would provide a better indicator of the PMI. A further study by Singh and colleagues (2006) on 311 cadavers in which the pericardial fluid was obtained between 2.5 and 58 hours after death was carried out. They found that there was a statistically significant, but not highly significant, correlation between the PMI and the rise in potassium and phosphate concentrations and the sodium/potassium ratio in pericardial fluid. Finally, a recent study by Kawamoto and colleagues (2013) analyzed a broad spectrum of electrolytes and proteins in postmortem pericardial fluid from 288 cadavers dying from a number of causes and diseases. In all cases there were moderate decreases in sodium and chloride and increases in potassium and magnesium which were not sufficient to correlate with the TSD but the authors found characteristic alterations in certain substances with certain causes of death which might be useful biomarkers to investigate the cause and process of death and to reinforce pathological and toxicological findings.

THE USE OF DNA AND RNA IN THE ESTIMATION OF THE PMI

Only a small number of papers dealing with research into deoxyribonucleic acid (DNA) and ribonucleic acid (RNA) degradation as a means of estimating the TSD have been published, and none of them has suggested its use as a quantitative method of estimating the PMI.

The autodegradation of DNA in human rib bone was investigated by Perry and colleagues (1988) to determine whether it was useful in estimating the TSD. It was found that variation in temperature affected the degradation rate, that there was some evidence that the DNA degradation rate was similar among different individuals, but that different bone from the same individual showed different rates of DNA degradation. DNA from bone marrow was degraded at a different rate from DNA in the bone cortex. The findings of Perry and colleagues indicated that DNA degradation was not useful in estimating the PMI.

Di Nunno and colleagues (1998) examined splenic cells in 35 cadavers from 24 to 126 hours after death to determine whether there was any correlation between DNA degradation and the time of death. Flow cytometry was used to evaluate DNA degradation in the cells. They found that although there was a precise correlation in the 24−36-hour period after death and a less precise correlation from 36 to 72 hours, the method was of no use after this time as the spleen autolyzed rapidly.

Johnson and Ferris (2002) discussed the analysis of postmortem DNA degradation by single-cell gel electrophoresis as a possible method of estimating the PMI. When cells die, nucleases are released that degrade chromosomal DNA into smaller fragments. Isolating, visualizing, and measuring the fragments might prove a quantifiable way of estimating the PMI. DNA fragmentation was studied in human leukocytes up to 22 hours after death and in pig tissues up to 72 hours. It was found that there was a process whereby nuclear DNA was fragmented following death, and this was organ- and time-dependent. Johnson and Ferris concluded that although the results showed a sequential, time-dependent process and potential for use as a future method of estimating the PMI, further studies were needed to determine the accuracy and precision and to determine the effect of varying temperature on the fragmentation process.

Bauer and colleagues (2003) studied postmortem RNA degradation, in order to determine whether quantification of the fragmentation of human mRNA might be useful as a method for the estimation of the PMI. They examined 50 postmortem blood samples and 36 brain tissue samples where the exact time of death was known. Fatty acid synthase−messenger RNA (FASN−mRNA) was chosen for analysis. Their results showed that RNA analysis from 50% of the postmortem blood samples failed to provide consistent results due to advanced hemolysis. In the remaining samples, FASN−mRNA molecules decreased continuously up to a PMI of 120 hours and the correlation was significant ($r = 0.808$). Analysis of brain samples showed a slow and continuous decrease in FASN−mRNA with time which was again significant ($r = 0.791$), but the error range was too large to justify the use of this method in medicolegal situations.

Several animal studies have shown good correlation between DNA fragmentation and the PMI (Liu et al., 2007; Chen et al., 2007; Mona et al., 2008; Gomaa et al., 2013) and with RNA fragmentation and the PMI (Sampaio-Silva et al., 2013). In contrast however a recent study of human rib bone samples taken within 24 hours post mortem and stored for varying periods of time from 103 to 445 days was carried out (Alaeddini et al., 2010). The samples were stored under four different conditions: freezing, ambient temperature, high humidity, and underground burial. DNA was extracted and examined for degradation. No correlation was found between DNA fragmentation and the PMI. At the present time the use of DNA and RNA for estimating the PMI remains in the experimental phase and is not of use in practice.

In a recent review of the use of postmortem biochemistry, Madea (2005) commented at length on the study of Di Nunno and colleagues. He criticized the study for the fact that it took no account of changes in body or ambient temperature, whereas previous German studies had shown that DNA degradation was faster in warmer than colder surroundings (Liebhart, 1969; Liebhart and Spann, 1973). Di Nunno and colleagues' study was also criticized because, as the authors had admitted, the proximity of the bowel to the spleen could have affected the degradation process by microbial migration during the autolytic process. Madea concluded that flow cytometric evaluation of DNA degradation was not yet a reliable or precise method of assessing the PMI. In general regarding biochemical methods of estimating the TSD, Madea stated that for practical purposes there was no real breakthrough because of the complex underlying metabolic processes involved in putrefaction and the estimation of the PMI by biochemical methods remained imprecise. He also stated that the importance of chemical methods could change in future if the following criteria were fulfilled: "quantitative measurement, mathematical description, taking into account influencing factors quantitatively, declaration of precision and proof of precision on independent material."

CONCLUSIONS

It appeared from an early stage that work on biochemical marker concentrations in closed compartments, protected for the most part from the confounding effects of autolysis in surrounding tissues, would be the ideal place to focus research into the PMI. Indeed the most intensively studied biochemical marker in PMI research has focused on the concentration of potassium in the vitreous humor. Nonstandardized methods, issues with study design, the variable effects of the state of samples (age, sex, ancestry, disease state) and the fact that the potassium concentration in living individuals (as well as its potential variability) is unknown have all contributed to the somewhat limited value of this means of estimating the TSD. Other biochemical markers within the vitreous humor of the eye, such as hypoxanthine for instance, have fared no better. Work on another closed compartment site, synovial fluid from joint compartments, although more difficult to extract and analyze, has also shown potassium concentrations to correlate with the PMI, which would indicate some degree of usefulness in estimating the TSD if vitreous fluid was unavailable for analysis. More generally, work on postmortem cell viability, enzyme activity, growth factor concentrations, immunological reactions as well as electrolyte concentrations in CSF and pericardial fluid have had for the most part positive results, but again not to the extent that they could be used in TSD estimation. Finally, work on quantifying DNA and RNA degradation post mortem has been proven to have no value in estimating the PMI.

REFERENCES

Abdel Salam, H.F., et al., 2012. Estimation of post-mortem interval using thanatochemistry and post-mortem changes. Alexandria J. Med. 48, 335–344.

Adelson, L., Sunshine, I., Rushforth, N.B., Mankoff, M., 1963. Vitreous potassium concentration as an indicator of post-mortem interval. J. Forensic Sci. 8 (4), 503–514.

Adjutantis, G., Coutselinis, A., 1972. Estimation of the time of death by potassium levels in vitreous humour. Forensic Sci. 1, 55–60.

Alaeddini, R., Walsh, S.J., Abbas, A., 2010. Molecular studies of time and environment dependent effects on bone DNA survival. Aust. J. Forensic Sci. 42 (3), 211–220.

Balasooriya, B.A.W., St Hill, C.A., Williams, A.R., 1984a. The biochemistry of vitreous humour. A comparative study of the sodium, potassium and urate concentrations in the eyes at identical time intervals after death. Forensic Sci. Int. 26, 85–91.

Balasooriya, B.A.W., St Hill, C.A., Williams, A.R., 1984b. The biochemical changes in pericardial fluid after death. An investigation of the relationship between the time since death and the rise or fall in electrolyte and enzyme concentrations and their possible usefulness in determining the time of death. Forensic Sci. Int. 26, 93–102.

Bardale, R., Dixit, P.G., 2007. Evaluation of morphological changes in blood cells of human cadaver for the estimation of post-mortem interval. Med-Leg. Update 7 (2), 35–39.

Bauer, M., Gramlich, I., Polzin, S., Patzelt, D., 2003. Quantification of mRNA degradation as possible indicator of post-mortem interval – a pilot study. Leg. Med. 5, 220–227.

Bocaz-Beneventi, G., et al., 2002. Capillary zone electrophoresis and artificial neural networks for estimation of the post mortem interval (PMI) using electrolytes measurements in human vitreous humour. Int. J. Legal Med. 116, 5–11.

Brinkman, B., May, D., Riemann, U., 1976. Postmortaler temperaturausgleich im bereich des kopfes. Z. Rechtsmed. 78, 69–82.

Chen, X., Yi, S., Liu, L., 2007. Image analysis for degradation of DNA in retinal nuclei of rat after death. J. Huazhong Univ. Sci. Technol. 27 (1), 24−26.

Coe, J.I., 1969. Post-mortem chemistries on vitreous humour. Am. J. Clin. Pathol. 51 (6), 741−750.

Coe, J.I., 1989. Vitreous potassium as a measure of the post-mortem interval: an historical review and critical evaluation. Forensic Sci. Int. 42, 201−213.

Coe, J.I., 1993. Post-mortem chemistry update. Am. J. Forensic Med. Pathol. 14 (2), 91−117.

Di Nunno, N.R., et al., 1998. Is flow cytometric evaluation of DNA degradation a reliable method to investigate the early post-mortem period?. Am. J. Forensic Med. Pathol. 19 (1), 50−53.

Dokgöz, H., Arican, N., Elmas, I., Fincanci, S.K., 2001. Comparison of morphological changes in white blood cells after death and in vitro storage of blood for the estimation of post-mortem interval. Forensic Sci. Int. 124, 25−31.

Duke-Elder, W.S., 1929. The physico-chemical properties of the vitreous body. J. Physiol. 68, 155−165.

Erlandsson, M., Munro, R., 2007. Estimation of the post-mortem interval in beagle dogs. Sci. Justice 47, 150−154.

Ferslew, K.F., Hagardorn, A.N., Travis Harrison, M., McCormick, W.F., 1998. Capillary ion analysis of potassium concentrations in human vitreous humour. Electrophoresis 19, 6−10.

Fineschi, V., et al., 1990. ^{1}H-NMR studies of post-mortem biochemical changes in rat skeletal muscle. Forensic Sci. Int. 44, 225−236.

Forbes, S.L., 2008. Forensic chemistry: applications to decomposition and preservation. In: Oxenham, M. (Ed.), Approaches to Death, Disaster and Abuse. Australian Academic Press, Brisbane, Ch. 15.

Gomaa, M.S., Abd El- Khalek, A.M., Sameer, M.M., 2013. The relationship between post-mortem interval and the DNA degradation in brain and liver of adult albino rats. J. Am. Sci. 9 (5), 535−540.

Gos, T., Raszeja, S., 1993. Post-mortem activity of lactate and malate dehydrogenase in human liver in relation to time after death. Int. J. Legal Med. 106, 25−29.

Hansson, L., Uotila, U., Lindfors, R., Laiho, K., 1966. Potassium content of the vitreous body as an aid in determination of time of death. J. Forensic Sci. 11 (3), 390−394.

Harkness, R.A., 1988. Hypoxanthine, xanthine and uridine in body fluids, indicators of ATP depletion. J. Chromatogr. 429, 255−278.

Henry, J.B., Smith, F.A., 1980. Estimation of the post-mortem interval by chemical means. Am J. Forensic Med. Pathol. 1 (4), 341−347.

Henssge, C., 1988. Death time estimation in case work. I. The rectal temperature time of death nomogram. Forensic Sci. Int. 38, 209−236.

Hjertén, S., 1967. Free zone electrophoresis. Chromatogr. Rev. 9, 122−219.

Hoffman, S.B., Morrow, G.W., Pease, G.L., Stroebel, C.F., 1964. Rate of cellular autolysis in post-mortem bone marrow. Am. J. Clin. Pathol. 41 (3), 281−286.

Hughes, W.M.H., 1965. Levels of potassium in the vitreous humour after death. Med. Sci. Law 5, 150−156.

Ith, M., et al., 2002a. Observation and identification of metabolites emerging during decomposition of brain tissue by means of in situ ^{1}H Magnetic Resonance Spectroscopy. Magn. Reson. Med. 48, 915−920.

Ith, M., et al., 2002b. Estimation of the post-mortem interval by means of [1]H-MR spectroscopy. Proc. Int. Soc. Magn. Reson. Med. 10 (Suppl.), 228.

Jaffe, F.A., 1962. Chemical post-mortem changes in the intraocular fluid. J. Forensic Sci. 7 (2), 231−237.

Johnson, L.A., Ferris, J.A.J., 2002. Analysis of post-mortem DNA degradation by single-cell gel electrophoresis. Forensic Sci. Int. 126, 43−47.

Kawamoto, O., Michiue, T., Ishikawa, T., Maeda, H., 2013. Comprehensive evaluation of pericardial biochemical markers in death investigation. Forensic Sci. Int. 224, 73−79.

Laiho, K., Penttilä, A., 1981. Autolytic changes in blood cells and other tissue cells of human cadavers. I. Viability and ion studies. Forensic Sci. Int. 17, 109−120.

Lange, N., Swearer, S., Sturner, W.Q., 1994. Human post-mortem interval estimation from vitreous potassium: an analysis of original data from six different studies. Forensic Sci. Int. 66, 159−174.

Leahy, M.S., Farber, E.R., 1967. Post-mortem chemistry of vitreous humour. J. Forensic Sci. 12 (2), 214−222.

Lie, J.T., 1967. Changes of the potassium concentration in the vitreous humour after death. Am. J. Med. Sci. 254 (2), 136−143.

Liebhart, E., 1969. Untersuchungen über das quantitative Verhalten der DNS in Abhängigkeit zu der seit dem Tode verstrichenen Zeit, Habilitation, Freiburg, Germany.

Liebhart, E., Spann, W., 1973. Cytophotometrische Untersuchungen zum Leichenalter. Beitr Grichtl Med. 30, 277−280.

Liu, L., et al., 2007. Determination of the early time of death by computerised image analysis of DNA degradation: which is the best quantitative indicator of DNA degradation? J. Huazhong Univ. Sci. Technol. 27 (4), 362−366.

Madea, B., 2005. Is there recent progress in the estimation of the post-mortem interval by means of thanatochemistry? Forensic Sci. Int. 151, 139−149.

Madea, B., Henssge, C., 2002. Eye changes after death. In: Knight, B. (Ed.), The Estimation of the Time since Death in the Early Post-mortem Period, second ed. Arnold, London, p. 103, Ch. 4.

Madea, B., Musshoff, F., 2007. Post-mortem biochemistry. Forensic Sci. Int. 165, 165−171.

Madea, B., Rödig, A., 2006. Time of death dependent criteria in vitreous humour − accuracy of estimating the time since death. Forensic Sci. Int. 164, 87−92.

Madea, B., Henssge, C., Hönig, W., Gerbracht, A., 1989. References for determining the time of death by potassium in vitreous humour. Forensic Sci. Int. 40, 231−243.

Madea, B., Herrmann, N., Henssge, C., 1990. Precision of estimating the time since death by vitreous potassium − comparison of two different equations. Forensic Sci. Int. 46, 277−284.

Madea, B., Käferstein, H., Hermann, N., Sticht, G., 1994. Hypoxanthine in vitreous humour and cerebrospinal fluid − a marker of post-mortem interval and prolonged (vital) hypoxia? Remarks also on hypoxanthine in SIDS. Forensic Sci. Int. 65, 19−31.

Madea, B., Kreuser, C., Banaschak, S., 2001. Post-mortem biochemical examination of synovial fluid − a preliminary study. Forensic Sci. Int. 118, 29−35.

Mason, J.K., Klyne, W., Lennox, B., 1951. Potassium levels in the cerebrospinal fluid after death. J. Clin. Pathol. 4, 231−233.

Mona, A. El-H., et al., 2008. The relationship between post-mortem interval and DNA degradation in different tissue of drowned rats. Mansoura J. Forensic Med. Clin. Toxicol. 16 (2), 45−60.

Muñoz, J.I., et al., 2001. A new perspective in the estimation of the post-mortem interval (PMI) based on vitreous [K^+]. J. Forensic Sci. 46 (2), 209−214.

Muñoz Barús, J.I., et al., 2002. Improved estimation of post-mortem interval based on differential behaviour of vitreous potassium and hypoxanthine in death by hanging. Forensic Sci. Int. 125, 67–74.

Naumann, H.N., 1959. Post-mortem chemistry of the vitreous body in man. Am. Med. Assoc. Arch. Ophthalmol. 62, 356–363.

Penttilä, A., Laiho, K., 1981. Autolytic changes in blood cells of human cadavers II. Morphological studies. Forensic Sci. Int. 17, 121–132.

Perry, W.L., Bass, W.A., Riggsby, W.S., Sirotkin, K., 1988. The autodegradation of deoxyribonucleic acid (DNA) in human rib bone and its relationship to the time interval since death. J. Forensic Sci. 33 (1), 144–153.

Petroff, O.A.C., Ogino, T., Alger, J.R., 1988. High resolution proton magnetic resonance spectroscopy of rabbit brain: regional metabolite levels and post-mortem changes. J. Neurochem. 51, 163–171.

Porteous, I.B., 1961. Persistence of motility in bone marrow cells from the cadaver. Nature 192 (4802), 569–570.

Pounder, D.J., Carson, D.O., Johnston, K., Orihara, Y., 1998. Electrolyte concentration differences between left and right vitreous humour samples. J. Forensic Sci. 43 (3), 604–607.

Reddy, D.V.N., Kinsey, V.E., 1960. Composition of the vitreous humour in relationship to that of plasma and aqueous humours. Arch. Ophthalmol. 83, 715.

Rognum, T.O., Hauge, S., Øyasaeter, S., Saugstad, O.D., 1991. A new biochemical method for estimation of post-mortem time. Forensic Sci. Int. 51, 139–146.

Sampaio-Silva, F., et al., 2013. Profiling of RNA degradation for estimation of post-mortem interval. PLoS One 8 (2), 1–8.

Saugstad, O.D., 1975. Hypoxanthine as a measure of hypoxia. Paediatr. Res. 9, 158–161.

Saugstad, O.D., Olaisen, B., 1978. Post-mortem hypoxanthine levels in the vitreous humour. An introductory report. Forensic Sci. Int. 12, 33–36.

Sheikh, N., 2007. Estimation of post-mortem interval according to time course of potassium ion activity in cadaveric synovial fluid. Ind. J. Forensic Med. Toxicol. 1 (1), 7–12.

Siddhamsetty, A.K., et al., 2014. Exploring time of death from potassium, sodium, chloride, glucose and calcium analysis of post-mortem synovial fluid in a semi-arid climate. J. Forensic Leg. Med. 28, 11–14.

Singh, D., Prashad, R., Sharma, S.K., Pandey, A.N., 2006. Estimation of post-mortem interval from human pericardial fluid electrolyte concentrations in Chandigarh zone of India: log transformed linear regression model. Leg. Med. 8, 279–287.

Stephens, R.J., Richards, R.G., 1987. Vitreous humour chemistry: the use of potassium concentration for the prediction of the post-mortem interval. J. Forensic Sci. 32 (2), 503–509.

Sturner, W.Q., 1963. The vitreous humour: post-mortem potassium changes. Lancet 281 (7285), 807–808.

Sturner, W.Q., Gantner, G.E., 1964. The post-mortem interval: a study of potassium in the vitreous humour. Am. J. Clin. Pathol. 42 (2), 137–144.

Tagliaro, F., et al., 1999. Capillary zone electrophoresis of potassium in vitreous humour: validation of a new method. J. Chromatogr. B 733, 273–279.

Tagliaro, F., et al., 2001. Potassium concentration differences in the vitreous humour from the two eyes revisited by microanalysis with capillary electrophoresis. J. Chromatogr. A 924, 493–498.

Tagliaro, F., Manetto, G., Crivellente, F., Smith, F.P., 1998. A brief introduction to capillary electrophoresis. Forensic Sci. Int. 92, 75–88.

Thaik-Oo, M., et al., 2002. Estimation of post-mortem interval from hypoxic inducible levels of Vascular Endothelial Growth Factor. J. Forensic Sci. 47 (1), 186–189.

Tumram, N.K., Bardale, R.V., Dongre, A.P., 2011. Post-mortem analysis of synovial fluid and vitreous humour for determination of death interval: a comparative study. Forensic Sci. Int. 204, 186–190.

Vass, A.A., et al., 1992. Time since death determinations in human cadavers using soil solution. J. Forensic Sci. 37 (5), 1236–1253.

Vass, A.A., et al., 2002. Decomposition chemistry of human remains: a new methodology for determining the post-mortem interval. J. Forensic Sci. 47 (3), 542–553.

Wehner, F., Wehner, H.-D., Schieffer, M.C., Subke, J., 1999. Delimitation of the time of death by immunohistochemical detection of insulin in pancreatic β cells. Forensic Sci. Int. 105, 161–169.

Wehner, F., Wehner, H.-D., Schieffer, M.C., Subke, J., 2000. Delimitation of the time of death by immunohistochemical detection of thyroglobulin. Forensic Sci. Int. 110, 199–206.

Wehner, F., Wehner, H.-D., Subke, J., 2001. Delimitation of the time of death by immuno-histochemical detection of calcitonin. Forensic Sci. Int. 122, 89–94.

Wyler, D., Marty, W., Bär, W., 1994. Correlation between the post-mortem cell content of cerebrospinal fluid and time of death. Int. J. Legal Med. 106, 194–199.

Yadav, J., et al., 2007. Estimation of time since death from C.S.F. electrolyte concentration in Bhopal region of central India. Leg. Med. 9, 309–313.

Research in the Later Stages of Decomposition

Human Body Decomposition. DOI: http://dx.doi.org/10.1016/B978-0-12-803691-4.00004-2

ESTIMATION OF THE POSTMORTEM INTERVAL DURING THE STAGE OF AUTOLYSIS AND EARLY PUTREFACTION

From the time a cadaver cools to ambient temperature and until it becomes a skeleton, soft tissue decomposes by aerobic and anaerobic bacterial action (Rodriguez and Bass, 1985). Autolysis, the disruption and disintegration of cell walls, varies depending on the surrounding environmental conditions but generally begins in bodies buried in graves at 48–72 hours after death (Dent et al., 2004). Intestinal cell membrane disruption releases aerobic and anaerobic bacteria. The process of autolysis gradually blends into the stage of decomposition known as putrefaction, which is characterized by decomposition occurring in an anaerobic environment (Gill-King, 1997). Decomposition is faster in the presence of oxygen, and therefore bodies on the surface decompose faster than those buried (Dent et al., 2004). The estimation of the postmortem interval (PMI) during this stage of decomposition is more difficult and less precise because of the multiple factors involved, which consist not only of intrinsic factors (ie, the physical and diseased state of the body) but also extrinsic factors (ie, the context in which the body decomposes). A body will decompose more rapidly if sepsis or a fever was present before death, in edematous tissues, in obese individuals, while decomposition will be slower in thin individuals and infants (Perper, 2006).

EXTRINSIC FACTORS AFFECTING DECOMPOSITION: TEMPERATURE, ENVIRONMENT, INSECTS, BURIAL, MOISTURE, SCAVENGING

The major extrinsic factor affecting decomposition is temperature, which affects not only the chemical processes controlling the enzymatic breakdown of proteins and carbohydrates but also the activity of insects and bacteria (Mann et al., 1990; Vass et al., 1992). Decomposition occurs more rapidly in air than in water or soil; it is more rapid in hot dry climates in summer than in winter (Galloway et al., 1989) and is slow in very cold climates (Komar, 1998). Twenty-nine bodies discovered decomposed in a number of contexts and over a widespread geographical area in Spain were studied by Prieto et al. (2004). Decomposition occurred more rapidly in cadavers in hot coastal regions of high humidity and where proliferation of microorganisms was greater, compared with inland regions where it was dryer and where there were more extreme seasonal changes in temperature. Cadavers found at high latitudes, where snow and ice occurred, decomposed even more slowly. Cadavers located outdoors decomposed more rapidly than those indoors or buried, while buried cadavers decomposed more rapidly than those in water. The authors concluded that insects, carnivores, high temperatures, and humidity were accelerants of the decomposition process, while low temperatures, burial, and submersion in water delayed decomposition.

Other extrinsic factors hastening decomposition are insects and animal scavenging. Together with temperature and burial depth, insects are the next most important variable, and influence the rate of decomposition by hastening tissue disintegration and the spread of bacteria (Mann et al., 1990; Payne, 1965; Simmons et al., 2010a). Animal scavenging is random, opportunistic, and occurs in both aquatic and terrestrial settings (Spradley et al., 2012; Steadman and Worne, 2007). Wilson and colleagues (2007) studied decomposing buried pigs and found that animal scavenging increased the rate of decomposition. Most studies of animal scavenging are case studies which do not advance research into the determination of the PMI (Steadman and Worne, 2007; Reeves, 2009).

Many factors affect the decomposition process in buried bodies. The deeper the burial, the slower is the decomposition (Rodriguez and Bass, 1985). The longer the burial, the greater the degree of decomposition, but there is no linear relationship between the burial time and stage of decomposition. Bodies buried in hot seasons decompose faster than those buried in colder seasons (Breitmeir et al., 2005). Soil type influences the rate of decomposition. In the previously mentioned study of Wilson and colleagues (2007), pigs were buried in pasture, deciduous woodland, and upland peat soil. Decomposition occurred most rapidly in pasture, less so in woodland and was slowest in upland moor soils. This was attributed to soil conditions such as moisture content, pH, and nutrient availability, which in turn controlled microbial numbers and activity at each site.

Carter and colleagues (2010) identified moisture as being the dominant environmental factor determining cadaver decomposition in soil. In their study, which was designed to test the hypothesis that an increase in moisture content of soil would result in a decrease in cadaver decomposition, rats were buried in a loam soil, a sandy soil, and a clay soil. The availability of moisture in soil is partly determined by the matric potential; specifically, the suction capacity of the soil for water, which in turn controls microbe motility, the diffusion of nutrients and waste, and the activity of extracellular enzymes. The matric potential is measured in megaPascals (MPa), and Carter et al. (2010) defined the matric potential of dry soil as being -0.3 MPa; moist soil -0.05 MPa; and wet soil -0.01 MPa. Microbial activity in soil was greatest at a matric potential of approximately -0.01 MPa. Clay, loam, and sandy soils, respectively, hold decreasingly less moisture (ie, the matric potential gradually increases). Cadaver decomposition increased with a decrease in matric potential (ie, it was more rapid in moister soils), but only to an optimal level (-0.01 MPa). The slower rate of decomposition in dry soils was not only due to restriction of microbe motility resulting from a lack of nutrient supply but also to the lack of moisture restricting the activity of enzymes, many of which were hydrolytic. In contrast, in very wet soils limited gas diffusion caused a decrease in aerobic metabolism and resulted in decreased decomposition.

DELAYED DECOMPOSITION AND PRESERVATION: MUMMIFICATION AND ADIPOCERE FORMATION

In certain environments, decomposition ceases and preservation of soft tissue occurs. Mummification is one such process, occurring in the whole body or parts of it when the environment is extremely dry (Forbes, 2008). Rapid desiccation of tissues inhibits enteric and soil bacterial action and can occur in very cold dry environments as well as very hot dry environments (Amy et al., 1986). The process of mummification is often a balance between putrefaction and dehydration with desiccation. Mummification can also occur naturally when bodies are preserved by the action of tannic acid in water, as occurs in bodies found in peat bogs (Aufderheide, 1981).

Bodies and body tissues may also be preserved by the formation of adipocere which is the postmortem conversion of fatty tissue into a solid material composed of saturated fatty acids, formed by the hydrolysis of triglycerides to free fatty acids which then undergo hydrogenation to saturated fatty acids such as myristic, palmitic, and stearic acids (Forbes et al., 2005). The process is aided by the actions of aerobic and anaerobic putrefactive bacteria (Forbes, 2008).

Conjugation of the fatty acids with bivalent metallic ions forms insoluble soaps of a hard consistency (Forbes, 2008). Fourcroy first described adipocere formation in exhumations from a Paris cemetery in 1789, gave it the name, and described it as a form of soap resulting from reactions of fat and ammonia (Ubelaker and Zarenko, 2011). Adipocere formation depends on the balance of a number of variable factors which include temperature, moisture, oxygen availability, soil type, method of burial, and the presence or absence of clothing (Ubelaker and Zarenko, 2011; Sledzik and Micozzi, 1997). Recent research has focused on the chemical formation of adipocere and its potential use, if any, in the determination of the PMI (Gotouda et al., 1988; Yan et al., 2001; Forbes et al., 2004; O'Brien and Kuehner, 2007).

In order to study the effect of the burial factors of soil pH, temperature, moisture, and oxygen content on the chemistry of adipocere formation, Forbes et al. (2004) buried 10 pigs in shallow graves. Fatty acid content was analyzed from cadaver tissue and from the soil beneath the cadavers. Fatty acids increased and were present in varying quantities at each of the stages of decomposition. There was a lack of correlation between the stage of adipocere formation and the decomposition interval, suggesting that the process was affected by factors in the environment other than the PMI, such as temperature, moisture, clothing, soil type, and pH. Accounting for these factors might better determine the correlation between the PMI and adipocere formation. In extending these studies, Forbes and colleagues (2005) investigated soil factors responsible for adipocere formation. Samples of pig flesh were buried in various types of soil to test the effects of soil pH, temperature, moisture, and oxygen content on the buried pig flesh. The control soil was a damp loamy sandy soil of pH 5.2. To test soil pH, samples of soil with pH 2.4 (acid), pH 8.5 (alkaline), and pH 12.6 (produced by adding lime) were tested. To test the effect of temperature, one sample was kept at 4°C and the other at 40°C. To test the effect of moisture, one sample was kept dry and the other wet. Finally, to test oxygen content, the control sample of soil was kept in an anaerobic environment while the other samples were all tested in an aerobic environment. Adipocere formation was found in most of the burial environments although the degree of formation varied. Factors favoring adipocere formation were a mildly alkaline pH, warm temperature, and anaerobic conditions, whereas factors inhibiting it were cold temperature, high alkalinity, and aerobic conditions. The highly acid soil did not entirely prevent adipocere formation but slowed it, possibly due to a lower bacterial load.

Most work into adipocere formation has been carried out with pigs, but research using pig and human adipose tissues, decomposing in similar controlled situations, found a difference in the rate of degradation between human and pig tissues (Notter et al., 2009). This difference was attributed to the variation of total fatty acid composition between species; pig adipose tissue has higher levels of total fatty acids than the same weight of human adipose tissue and therefore adipocere formation occurs sooner in the decomposition process in pigs than in human tissue. Variations in the amount of sodium, potassium, calcium, and magnesium were also detected between species.

Ubelaker and Zarenko (2011) stated that adipocere represents a chemical form of mummification and that it can form in a variety of environments, both aquatic and terrestrial. It can form shortly after death and be present for hundreds of years. Factors favorable for the formation of adipocere are the presence of body fat, moisture, mildly alkaline pH, warm temperature, anaerobic conditions, and the appropriate bacteria. Aerobic conditions and Gram-positive bacteria will aid in its degradation.

Both mummification and adipocere formation complicate attempts to more accurately determine the PMI by preserving tissue and delaying decomposition. Some tentative research has been carried out into determining the PMI in early mummified cadavers by estimating the ion ratios leaching into soil beneath a cadaver (Vass et al., 1992). At the present time research into the chemical changes occurring in adipocere formation as a means of determining the PMI is in the very early stage (Ubelaker and Zarenko, 2011).

ESTIMATION OF THE PMI IN THE LATER STAGES OF PUTREFACTION AND SKELETONIZATION

Forensic Entomology and the Estimation of the PMI

Forensic entomology is a specialty within forensic science with an extensive and growing volume of literature. The first documented case of insects being used in a forensic case is that of Sung Tz'u, in mid-13th-century China (see also chapter: Supravital Reactions in the Estimation of the

Time Since Death (TSD)) who investigated the case of a man found dead by a roadside (Sung Tz'u, 1186–1249). The man had not been robbed but had 10 wounds inflicted by a sickle. After making inquiries of the man's wife, Sung Tz'u went to the neighborhood of a man suspected of being the perpetrator of the crime and demanded that all the nearby owners of sickles lay them on the ground. The weather was hot and the murderer was identified as being the owner of the only sickle with blood staining on it, to which flies flocked. The first modern recorded case using insects in a forensic investigation was in France when Dr Bergeret, in a report dated 1855, described attempts to determine the time of death of a baby from the fly eggs, larvae, and pupae as well as moth pupae deposited on the body (Benecke, 2001). In the 1920s the first case studies of important forensic insect species began to be published and, importantly, it was recognized that blowflies colonized open wounds on cadavers, resulting in more rapid decomposition, but that insects failed to colonize mummified cadavers (Benecke, 2001). Only since the 1980s has entomology developed as a widespread forensic tool in Australia (Wallman, 2002).

In the class of insects, the blowfly family in the order Diptera, has a worldwide distribution and is the most forensically important insect family with which the PMI is determined, because the lifecycle of the blowfly is intimately tied to carrion (Wallman, 2002). They are the first insect to colonize a cadaver, attracted by the odors and gases exuded by decaying organic matter and the colonization, egg laying (oviposition), and subsequent growth and development depend on environmental factors, the most important of which are temperature and ease of access to the cadaver (Mann et al., 1990; Campobasso ct al., 2001). After blowflies, house flies (family Muscidae) and flesh flies (family Sarcophagidae) colonize a body at the bloated stage. There follows a succession of fly and beetle families that are then attracted to the body during the various stages of decay, by rancid fats and ammoniacal fermentation (Campobasso et al., 2001; Rodriguez and Bass, 1983). Body orifices are often the first area to be colonized followed by moist flexure creases, as the maggots move to areas of more favorable food opportunities (Campobasso et al., 2001). The eggs develop into larvae or maggots, which go through three stages of development known as instars during which time the morphology changes with growth and the passage of time. The skin of the maggots hardens and they form pupae, which later form into adult flies. The growth rate is faster when the environmental temperature is high, when there is increased temperature generated from bacterial action during decay and when temperature rises as a result of the growing maggot mass (Simmons et al., 2010a; Rivers et al., 2011). Blowflies mainly lay eggs in daylight, although they have been known to do so in artificial light and temperature is the main factor in their growth and development (Campobasso et al., 2001). There is a temperature range which is optimum for blowfly larvae to develop and the range varies with each species. Below a certain temperature embryogenesis in eggs and larval development will slow down or cease but may resume or speed up as temperatures again rise (Campobasso et al., 2001). Above a certain temperature larval feeding is inhibited, development of pupae slows, and if the temperature is too high certain toxic proteins developing in the larvae may prove to be lethal (Rivers et al., 2011). Maggot masses produce a rise in temperature dependent on the size of the maggot mass and the size of the cadaver (Campobasso et al., 2001). The cause of the temperature rise is unknown but has been attributed to microbial activity, frenetic muscular movement of the mass, and high metabolism associated with digestive processes (Rivers et al., 2011) and it has been known to reach very high levels (Anderson and Van Laerhoven, 1996).

After temperature, access to the body by insects is the next most important factor affecting decomposition (Mann et al., 1990). The absence of blowfly and beetle activity, occurring in certain environmental conditions which prevent insect access; burial of a body, excessive clothing cover, and excessively cold temperatures will delay decomposition. The deeper a body is buried the more limited is insect access and in burials deeper than 60 cm there is no sign of carrion insect activity (Rodriguez and Bass, 1985; Campobasso et al., 2001). Similarly there is a different array of insect species which colonize a cadaver found indoors compared with one found outdoors (Goff, 1991). Recent studies from southern Finland and Canada found that indoor carcasses were colonized more slowly by blowflies and that decomposition was slower than that occurring in carcasses situated outdoors (Pohjoismäki et al., 2010; Anderson, 2011). In the Finnish study, which studied human remains, different species of insects colonized cadavers decomposing indoors, compared with the species which colonized cadavers decomposing outdoors (Pohjoismäki et al., 2010). An average delay of 3−4 days occurred before the first female blowflies found the indoor cadavers and oviposited. This was attributed to more difficult access to the indoor cadavers, time of year, cooler temperatures, and the species reserves of the local insects. In the Canadian study using pig carcasses, there was a 5-day delay before indoor carcasses were colonized (Anderson, 2011). Many more insects colonized the outdoor carcasses and these were more rapidly skeletonized.

Not all insects which colonize a cadaver actively consume decomposing tissue; some species are opportunists or parasites of other species. Goff (1993) classified the insects attracted to decomposing cadavers into four categories:

1. Necrophagous species are those directly feeding on the cadaver. Diptera (Calliphoridae and Sarcophagidae) and Coleoptera (Silphidae and Dermestidae) are the dominant species in this category.
2. Predators and parasites of the necrophagous species which include other species of Coleoptera and Calliphoridae and also Hymenoptera. Some Diptera larvae become predators in the later stage of their development.
3. Omnivorous species such as wasps, ants, and some beetles which feed on the corpse as well as the necrophagous species. Large numbers of these may delay decomposition by excessively consuming the necrophagous species.
4. Adventive species use the corpse as an extension of their normal habitat and include spiders and centipedes.

While biochemical and temperature methods of determining the PMI may give reasonable results up to about 1–3 days after death, entomological evidence may extend the estimation of the PMI up to several weeks or even months (Amendt et al., 2007). From 48 hours after death forensic entomology is frequently the only way of determining the PMI with any degree of accuracy (Wallman, 2002).

The minimum PMI (mPMI) in the first days after death is based on the age assessment of the oldest immature stages of necrophagous insects (eggs, larvae, or pupae) on the body, mainly blowflies, the first insects to infest a cadaver, which in turn depends on the species and their particular rate of growth. This age assessment will indicate a mPMI, corresponding with the time that the insects first colonized the body but it may not correspond with the actual time of death as the period of insect activity may be less than the PMI. The reason for this is that blowflies may have either not colonized the body immediately after death because of difficulty of access or they may have colonized the body before death if necrotic tissue had been available in a debilitated and dying individual (Amendt et al., 2007). Later in the postmortem period the mPMI is based on the composition of the insect community; different insect species infest a body at different times during its decomposition, as the activity of each successive species renders the body unsuitable for continuing occupation by itself (Wallman, 2002). Age assessment of the oldest immature specimens will depend on correct identification of the predominant local species and environmental conditions. Studies such as those of Anderson and Van Laerhoven (1996), Wallman (2001), and Archer and Elgar (2003), which determine the predominant species in a particular geographical area, are important in providing a reference database of blowfly species for forensic cases including measurements of length and weight of the larval instars (Amendt et al., 2007). Identification of the different species of blowflies is made more accurate by examining the microscopic morphology of mouth parts, posterior body spiracles, and by molecular identification of proteins expressed by the DNA within cells, the DNA itself, or the mitochondrial DNA (Harvey et al., 2003; Wallman et al., 2005). The later stages of pupae and adults can also be aged by measuring the stages of development and comparing them with tables relating development to temperature (Amendt et al., 2007). Various arthropod succession patterns have been used to determine the PMI after blowflies have migrated from a body, in one case up to 36 days (Goff and Flynn, 1991) but when using the greater carrion insect community in forensic investigations it is necessary to have knowledge of local successional patterns based on experimental studies on animal carcasses such as pigs (Amendt et al., 2007).

As growth rate and development are dependent on temperature, the quantitative amount of heat required is measured in accumulated degree hours (ADH) or accumulated degree days (ADD). ADD was originally introduced by Arnold (1959) over 50 years ago as a thermal unit measure, although Réaumur (1735) developed the concept of heat units with reference to plant development in the 18th century (Wang, 1960) (see an extended discussion of the use of ADD in chapter: Recent Research and Current Trends). The use of these measures was subsequently promoted by Edwards and Chaney, who defined a degree day as "the amount of biological activity caused by 1 degree above the threshold for 1 day" (Edwards et al., 1987). Amendt et al.

(2007) defined ADH and ADD as the temperature in degrees Centigrade above base temperature multiplied by time either in hours or days. The use of these measurements is based on the assumption that under a constant temperature there is a linear relationship between temperature and growth and development. The base or threshold temperature is the temperature below which development ceases and this, and the temperature range which is optimal, varies for each developmental stage and each species of blowfly in different geographical areas (Amendt et al., 2007; Edwards et al., 1987). If the temperature range fluctuates the development may become less linear. The recording of hourly temperature at the site of body discovery for 5 or 10 days afterwards, with a data logger, is carried out. Temperature records for the actual time the body lay in situ are obtained from the nearest local weather station. A regression equation is then calculated from which a corrective factor is obtained and applied to the weather station readings in order to compensate for the geographical distance between the body discovery site and the weather station (Amendt et al., 2007). A study by Archer (2004) found that although the accuracy of temperature data at particular sites was usually improved by correction factors, the degree of improvement was highly variable between correlation periods, therefore generous error margins of at least ± 12 hours should be quoted and in some cases should be even much longer. Johnson et al. (2012) expanded on the 2004 study. They found that although retrospective ambient temperature correction of weather station temperature was a robust technique and was not significantly affected by season, corrected weather data were less representative of actual body detection site temperatures if correlation was attempted when there was a temperature difference of $>5°C$ between the weather station collection data and the correlation data from the body discovery site. In such a case they recommended a collection of 10 days of correlation data in order to extend the correlation period to try to correct any difference exceeding $5°C$ between weather station data and the body detection site data.

Isomegalen reference curves, which give insect growth stages for various constant temperatures and isomorphen diagrams, which document morphological development depending on time and temperature, have been developed to aid the correlation of age and morphology with temperature but should be developed for the same and different species in different geographical areas (Grassberger and Reiter, 2001).

Strict, universally recognized, and consistent standards are also necessary for collecting, storing, and assessing insect species in order that legal requirements are met and studies can be compared (Amendt et al., 2007).

Insects are not only important in determining the mPMI but have been shown, together with temperature and burial depth, to be the most important factors affecting the rate of decay in bodies (Mann et al., 1990). Payne (1965) had noted this fact in a study of decomposition of baby pigs and it was further confirmed by Rodriguez and Bass (1983), when they studied insect successions on four human cadavers decomposing in different seasons of the year. They noticed that during autumn and winter, when insect populations were at their minimum, decomposition occurred more slowly. They concluded that insects were a major factor responsible for decomposition. In a study on groups of rabbits decomposing on the surface of the ground, some being disturbed at intervals while others were left undisturbed, it was found that the undisturbed group lost weight, their body temperature was greater, and they decomposed faster than the disturbed group (Adlam and Simmons, 2007). Temperature over the 3-week study period was measured as ADDs and correlated with the stage of decomposition, which was measured by a quantitative scoring system. The faster rate of decomposition in the undisturbed group was attributed to higher temperatures reached as a result of an increase in blowfly numbers, which in turn resulted in a greater maggot mass and consequently, to a faster rate of decomposition.

In a recent study using a quantitative body scoring system to measure decomposition and ADDs to measure temperature over the time of decomposition, Bachmann and Simmons (2010) showed that soft tissue decomposition was significantly faster in a group of 30 rabbit carcasses exposed to insects for 5 hours prior to shallow burial, than in a group of 30 rabbit carcasses which had insects excluded by storing them in plastic bags at 4°C during transportation, the bags being removed just before immediate burial. Both groups of rabbits were buried at the same time.

Simmons and colleagues (2010b) undertook an analysis of a number of published and unpublished studies using rats, rabbits, pigs, and humans in varying environments. Only studies in which it was possible to convert the timescale to ADDs were chosen.

Decomposition had previously been shown to correlate with weight loss (Adlam and Simmons, 2007). If weight loss data were reported in a study as a percentage, they were converted into a total body score (TBS) by using a specific formula. By this means Simmons and colleagues were able to compare ADDs with TBS and found that, regardless of the environment, cadavers with insect access decomposed at a faster rate than cadavers when insects were excluded. When insects were present small carcasses decomposed faster than large carcasses, which the authors explained by there being more mass for the insects to consume but when insects were excluded carcass size had no influence on the decomposition rate.

Forensic entomology is therefore a recent but increasingly important and developing specialty within forensic science which has increasing potential to be of assistance in more accurately estimating the TSD in decomposed human bodies, especially after the first 48 hours after death (Wallman, 2002). Its importance will increase with the number of studies carried out to identify the different species of blowflies and other arthropods, their development, and behavior in different geographical areas (Wallman, 2001; Archer and Elgar, 2003; Anderson, 2000; Matuszewski et al., 2008, 2010a,b).

ESTIMATION OF THE PMI IN SKELETAL REMAINS

The estimation of the PMI of a cadaver decomposed to a skeleton is much more difficult and inaccurate. In the United Kingdom it is generally accepted that human bones in which the date of death is estimated to be greater than approximately 75 years are treated as historical cases, whereas bones with a date of death less than 75 years are investigated as forensic cases although this cut-off date varies in different jurisdictions throughout the world (Swift, 2006; Yoshino et al., 1991). The methods available can be categorized as indirect and direct (Swift, 2006; Knight and Lauder, 1969).

Indirect Methods

Botanical knowledge may assist in determining the PMI with buried bodies or bodies which have lain in the open for a long time. Palynology (pollen and spores analysis) may indicate the season when the remains were deposited (Swift, 2006) and assessment of the roots of perennial plants growing through or around the body by dendrochronology may give a minimum TSD (Willey and Heilman, 1987). Assessment may be difficult because the seasonal rate of growth may vary with the environmental conditions. Roots growing vertically through the remains make assessment more accurate than those growing horizontally or obliquely. Difficulties occur with false rings, incomplete rings, and eccentric rings. Roots of annual plants make assessment more accurate, as they indicate deposition of the body in that season. Despite these disadvantages the method can sometimes be very useful as a recent case from Canada indicates (Courtin and Fairgrieve, 2004). A decomposed body was found dressed in winter clothes in a wooded area, lying on the ground across the branch of a North American black spruce. As this tree grows, the lower branches dip on to the ground and then subsequently grow up to the light. The body had fallen over a branch as it lay on the ground and the branch had then grown upwards over several years. The weight of the body on the branch had compressed the annual growth rings on the side of the branch closest to the ground. By microscopically measuring and counting the number of compressed rings, it was established that the person had died 10 years previously and this was confirmed by further investigation.

Direct Methods
Morphological Examination
In the early stage of skeletonization, ligaments and tendons may remain attached and bone marrow, periosteum, and the collagenous framework may persist in long bones. These features might be thought to give an estimate of the PMI but they are dependent on the environment in which the body was found, for example, acid soil will cause decomposition of these structures rapidly, while rapid immersion in anoxic water and rapid burial in sediment will preserve them for longer periods (Schultz, 1997; White and Hannus, 1983). Other factors such as animal scavenging will obscure these features (Spradley et al., 2012). Behrensmeyer (1978) studied the bones of mammals deposited in the Amboseli Basin of Kenya, described the weathering processes, and produced a timetable of weathering based on these descriptions up to 10−15 years after death by which time most bones had decomposed beyond recognition. Behrensmeyer concluded that weathering processes might record useful information but much more research was required. Research by White and Hannus (1983), who analyzed the chemical changes in bone as it weathered, illustrated the complexity of

the process. Estimation of the PMI from the morphology of skeletal material is one of the most important, yet unreliable aspects of forensic investigation. It is dependent on the experience of the examiner, which is open to observer error and lack of corroborative evidence (Swift et al., 2001).

Microscopic Examination
A study by Knight and Lauder (1969) was undertaken in an attempt to determine the dating of skeletal remains and in particular to determine a method of distinguishing modern from ancient bone. Several methods were researched including histology, but the authors concluded that histology was technically impossible on many of the bones and unless undecalcified sectioning became available, it was not worth performing.

In a study by Yoshino and colleagues (1991), 51 bone fragments from the surgical necks of humeri were studied by light microscopy and electron microscopy. Of these, 33 were left in the open air, 14 were buried, and 4 were left in the sea for several years. Specimens buried in soil showed changes beginning after 5–10 years. Vacuoles first formed in the bone, which then coalesced to form labyrinthine structures. Their walls were formed by thin collagen fibrils along which bacteria could be seen. Similar changes were seen in bones exposed in the open and in the sea. However, the changes in bones in the open took many more years to develop and the changes in the bones in the sea did not develop into labyrinthine cavities but remained at the stage of vacuole formation. The researchers concluded that the labyrinthine structures were formed by bacteria breaking down the walls of the vacuoles and that the bacteria attacked both the organic and inorganic components of the bone. They were unable to formulate a quantifiable method of estimating the PMI from these microscopic changes.

Bell and colleagues (1996) studied human bones from three environments, terrestrial, lakes, and the sea, in order to assess the speed of postmortem alteration to bone. Specimens were mainly of ribs and teeth, with one tibial shaft. The PMI was known approximately and extended from 3 months to 83 years. Sections were cut, treated, and examined by scanning electron microscope. The authors confirmed the changes described by Yoshino et al. (1991) but found that they could occur very soon after death and up to many years after. Too few specimens were examined to enable a TSD to be established but the authors favored endogenous bacteria associated with the body for causing the bone breakdown rather than exogenous bacteria associated with the environment.

A detailed histological study of the femoral bones of 12 pig carcasses was carried out by White and Booth (2014) in order to determine whether the bacteria responsible for postmortem degradation of bone were endogenous gut bacteria or exogenous from the environment. There were 10 juvenile pigs and 2 stillborn. Five juveniles and a stillborn were buried in a shallow grave; the remainder were exposed in the open air for a year. Decomposition was staged on each carcass but no correlation was found with the histological changes in bone. Bone histology was similar to that noted by Yoshino and colleagues. White and Booth (2014) concluded that enteric bacteria were responsible for consuming the microstructure and would probably alter most of the internal bone structure within 5 years. Cadavers on the surface showed more bone destruction than buried cadavers and stillborn pig bones remained free of destruction because of the lack of enteric bacteria. The findings of these studies are interesting in elucidating the cause and timing of postmortem bone destruction but do not yet aid in the development of a method of estimating the TSD.

METHODS MEASURING PHYSICOCHEMICAL CHANGES

Knight and Lauder (1967) investigated a number of physicochemical methods of dating 11 specimens of bone, the dates of which were approximately known and which varied from 0 to 1700 years. The methods were fluorescence under ultraviolet light, estimation of nitrogen content, benzidine reaction, immune-electrophoresis, paper chromatography of the amino acid content, Nile blue and dichloroindophenol staining, and reaction with acid. The methods used were useful in distinguishing ancient from modern bone. Recently deposited bone was distinguished by a nitrogen content of more than 4 g%, a positive benzidine reaction on powdered bone and the production of seven or more amino acids on hydrolysis as demonstrated by paper chromatography. Loss of immunologic activity occurred after 5 years and benzidine staining after 150 years. Fluorescence was of limited value, effervescence of the bone surface with acid was of no value, and neither was Nile blue and dichloroindophenol staining. Further studies since then have researched various methods and these include the following.

Nitrogen and Albumin Levels in Bones

Nitrogen levels in bones from 42 bodies buried in coffins in two cemeteries with similar soil profiles for periods which varied from 26 to 93 years were examined by Jarvis (1997). Quicklime had been added to 17 of the coffins and there was fuel oil contamination of 3 coffins. Total nitrogen concentration of the long bones was analyzed and found to decrease with time. The relationship could be expressed by a regression equation when the confounding effect of other variables was removed. Below 4 feet (1.22 m), the depth of the shallowest burial, the depth made no difference to the nitrogen content, neither did the presence of lime. Three bodies contaminated with fuel oil had higher nitrogen levels, and a skeleton found in the open on the surface after 14 years had a nitrogen level much less than the average nitrogen level in the buried bodies.

Lowenstein (1981) reported that collagen, the principal protein of bone, had been detected by electron microscopy in dinosaurs 200 million years old. Using antisera to albumin as a control, he developed a solid-phase radioimmunoassay for collagen, albumin, and other proteins and he discovered that serum factors as well as collagen could survive in fossil extracts from a baby mammoth, an Egyptian mummy, as well as in such hominids as Cro-Magnon, Neanderthal, *Homo erectus*, and *Australopithecus robustus*. Cattaneo and colleagues (1992) demonstrated that human albumin could be identified in bone, with good sensitivity and specificity, by inhibition enzyme-linked immunosorbent assay (ELISA) using a monoclonal antibody of the Ig class against human albumin. They successfully identified albumin in human bone from 2200 to 1700 BC, from skeletons dating from the English Civil War in AD 1644, from medieval (AD 1100–1400), early Saxon (AD 450–600), Roman (AD 100–200), and from Iron Age bone (400 BC). The results were unequivocal with no crossreactivity between humans and other species. The authors suggested that the method provided a means to reconstruct dietary, ritual, and domestic practices of ancient peoples but the method was not suggested to estimate the TSD. Swift (2006), in his review of the use of nitrogen levels in estimating the PMI, concluded that although the amino acid content of bone, from which nitrogen is derived, may alter in a somewhat recognizable manner, the rate of decrease was unpredictable and it was prone to alteration by too many external factors such as fertilizers in soil, to be of practical use in the estimation of the PMI.

Ultraviolet Fluorescence

The use of ultraviolet fluorescence of bone as a method of determining the age of bones was investigated by Facchini and Pettener (1977). A bluish white fluorescence occurs when bone is subjected to ultraviolet light and this is caused by the presence of organic constituents. As bone ages it gradually loses these constituents and, theoretically, the intensity and distribution of the fluorescence should diminish. It was suggested that if fluorescence diminished in a linear manner it might indicate the PMI. Seventy-one specimens of adult femora, varying from just over 20 years to 3500 years old, were subjected to ultraviolet light after being finely sectioned. A spectrofluorimeter was used to quantitatively measure the ultraviolet light emitted. Samples were classified by age into recent (AD 1935−1945), modern (AD 1600−1800), medieval (AD 700−1000), Roman (AD 100−300), Etruscan (540−450 BC), archaic (600−500 BC), and ancient Bronze Age (1700−1500 BC) groups. Fluorescence, when ultraviolet light was applied, was widespread over the surface of bones up to 200−350 years old, discontinuous and weaker in medieval samples, and absent in older bones. Quantitative differences in fluorescence intensity were noted in the modern samples but it was not significant. The authors concluded that fluorescence was too variable to be used as a reliable dating method.

Yoshino and colleagues (1991), found that ultraviolet fluorescence of bones diminished with time in a sample up to 15 years after death. They calculated regression equations to date the bone, but the standard error of all samples was 2.223 years and the confidence interval at 5% was 4.5 years.

A study by Hoke and colleagues (2011) visually determined the UV-induced autofluorescence of the cross-sections from 76 horse bone fragments dating from 15,000 to 2000 BC from prehistoric archeological sites of varying environmental and chronological background. In each sample they compared the fluorescence with the degree of histological preservation, itself a marker for overall biomolecular preservation in bone. They concluded that the relationship between fluorescence and unaltered microstructure appeared to be good and that screening samples with fluorescence could help identify samples with the best chances for collagen and DNA recovery. UV fluorescence was also faster and less elaborate than the histological method. However, the general cause of the fluorescence and exactly what caused the specific changes in color in degraded bone was still not known. Finally, a recent study by Hoke and colleagues (2013) examined 213 bones from two sets of bones with a known PMI in order to determine the diagnostic value of ultraviolet fluorescence in distinguishing historical and recent skeletal remains. The first set was 58 long bone samples from abandoned graves in a modern cemetery ranging from 8 to 60 years after death. The second set was 155 archeological specimens from different sites throughout Germany. There were 76 horse bones ranging from 2000 to 15,000 years after death and 79 human bones ranging from 90 to 4500 years after death. They concluded that the use of ultraviolet fluorescence in distinguishing between a forensically relevant and a historical PMI was questionable and specifically the intensity of fluorescence did not show a significant correlation with the PMI.

The fluorescence of bone under ultraviolet light is considered to be caused by residual organic constituents, mainly collagen (Facchini and Pettener, 1977). Loss of collagen from bone is not only caused by microbial degradation but it is also temperature-dependent and both these causes depend on environmental conditions (Hedges, 2002). Therefore, loss of collagen from bone is highly variable and hence estimation of the PMI by ultraviolet fluorescence will also be variable. These studies indicate that the use of bone fluorescence is not sufficiently accurate to estimate the PMI in forensic cases.

Benzidine Staining

Facchini and Pettener (1977) investigated the use of benzidine staining in bone. The application of benzidine in acetic acid with the later addition of hydrogen peroxide will stain any residual blood pigment in the bone blue. Strong positive results were found in recently deceased samples, weaker reactions in modern bones, but medieval and Roman bones only gave false-positive results due to iron staining resulting from burial environment soils. Facchini and Pettener concluded that the intensity of staining could date remains from 0 to 350 years. Benzidine is carcinogenic; its use has been replaced by aminobenzidine and the method gives too many false-positive results to be useful (Swift, 2006).

Chemiluminescence

Introna and colleagues (1999) investigated luminol, an alkaline reagent for its potential in estimating the PMI from bone. Luminol is routinely used in forensic serology to locate and identify blood traces and stains which are not visible to the naked eye and it is very sensitive. Luminol produces a bluish-white light when peroxidase is added to it in the presence of blood and it is the heme portion of hemoglobin that reacts with the peroxidase. The color and intensity of the light can be measured. Samples of bone from 80 nonpathological femurs were subjected to luminol testing. The samples, from 40 males and 40 females, were grouped into five time periods according to the known time of death, but with sufficient intervals to prevent overlaps in the positive results from the tests. The time periods were 1 month to 3 years, 10−15 years, 25−35 years, 50−60 years, and greater than 80 years. A camera recorded the chemiluminescence and brightness was measured by a computer software program (Olivetti PC PRO 486/33 MHz-8MbRAM). The test was always positive and intense in bones from the first group; 80% of the second group showed luminescence visible to the eye but luminescence gradually reduced in positivity and brightness as the PMI increased. After a PMI of 25 years it was negative in 70% and after 50 years only 10% were positive. Introna and colleagues suggested that the luminol test could be useful in determining the TSD from skeletal remains, especially when only isolated or fragmented bones were recovered, but it should be tested on a wider sample of bones with a closer PMI range in order to establish its statistical significance.

In another study by Ramsthaler and colleagues (2009), 80 powdered bone samples from four known historical periods were tested with the naked eye by two independent observers in randomized, blind experiments by chemiluminescence with luminol. Technical aids such as cameras and light detectors were deliberately not used. The historical periods were: 1st−3rd centuries AD, 1878−1902, 1965−1972, and 1995−2003. Observer error was corrected statistically; assessing luminescence was simplified by visualization in a dark room and reported as being either present or absent. False-positive and false-negative results were used as the main criteria for assessing the method. A false-positive result was the error of classifying a historical bone as recent, and a false-negative was the error of rejecting a modern bone as being historical, a potentially worse error, as forensic cases could thereby be left unexamined. The results were observer-independent but unexpected results occurred in 7.5% of all historical cases and 15% of recent samples were false-negatives. A correct classification occurred in 88.75%. False-positive results occurred in 7.5% and false-negative results in 10% of cases. Ramsthaler and colleagues concluded that chemiluminescence on its own was not adequate for distinguishing between recent and nonrecent skeletal remains. An estimation of the PMI using the luminol test alone was also not possible without interpreting environmental and anthropological factors, and additional methods of estimating the PMI should be used in conjunction with this test.

A further study by Ramsthaler and colleagues (2011) compared the use of ultraviolet fluorescence, luminol, Hexagon-OBTI, and Combur tests to determine the PMI in skeletal remains by the detection of intraosseous hemin traces. The Hexagon-OBTI test is based on an antibody reaction to human hemoglobin and hemoglobin breakdown products such as hemin and is used to detect blood in feces. It can detect levels of 0.88 mg Hb/g of feces. Combur is a commercial chemical incorporated in a test strip, and it is even more sensitive in detecting the same hemoglobin products than the Hexagon-OBTI test. The hypothesis underlying the research was that the chemiluminescence of the luminol reaction was due to the presence of persisting hemin from hemoglobin molecules in bone and that this was related to the PMI. The researchers also wished to test whether or not the Hexagon-OBTI and the Combur methods of testing for chemiluminescence were more effective. Sample long bones from 39 individuals with known PMIs varying from 0 to 2500 years were tested with the three methods. UV fluorescence could exclude bones with a forensically relevant PMI of less than 50 years, but only if reduction in reflection was marked. Eight percent of the samples with a PMI less than 100 years tested negative for the luminol reaction, while 35% with a PMI over 100 years tested positive. The sample size was small and burial conditions may have influenced the results.

Ramsthaler and colleagues concluded that a negative luminol test, which indicated a PMI without forensic relevance, was superior to a positive luminol test indicating a short PMI (ie, less than 50 years) which might be forensically relevant. None of the bones tested positive to the Hexagon-OBTI or Combur tests despite all controls testing positive. The authors concluded that the Hexagon-OBTI and Combur tests were not suitable for estimating or reducing the error of estimation of the PMI at present, but they were unable to reach a satisfactory reason for the failure of these methods. They suggested that further research was required to determine whether the bone samples were dissolved for a sufficient length of time in the buffer solution used for these tests, or if the hemoglobin was sufficiently soluble in the buffer solution.

Citrate Content of Bone

Recently a method of measuring the citrate content of bone as a means of estimating the PMI was reported by Schwarcz et al. (2010). Citrate, a tricarboxylic acid, is a key component of the Krebs cycle which is essential to the metabolism of all cells. About 90% of the citrate in the body is present in bone at a constant concentration of between 1.5% and 2% by weight and its purpose is thought to be to prevent excessive growth of hydroxyapatite crystals which are essential to the structure of all newly formed bone. While there are differences in concentration between different types of bone, the concentration within each type is constant in all adults regardless of sex and age. However, the citrate concentration may depend on the state of bone mineralization and may therefore be lower in immature and osteoporotic bone. Corresponding skeletal components in other vertebrates, such as cows and pigs, also contain almost identical citrate, showing that uptake of citrate from blood is a general characteristic of all bone and not restricted to humans. Therefore animal bones could be used in studies as proxies for human bones. Schwarcz and colleagues quoted an unpublished study which found that citrate content in bone buried for more than 100 years was less than 1% of the initial content. If the loss of citrate was gradual it could be used as a forensic tool to determine the PMI and a study was designed to determine whether the citrate content of bone could be used as an estimate of the TSD.

Samples of pig and human rib bones were placed in different contexts: buried, on the ground, and under glass jars. Some of these samples were human bone forensic specimens from a number of locations and different contexts across North America. Some of the buried bones and some from under the glass jars were lifted and frozen to determine the extent to which the climate or storage environment might influence the loss of citrate. The citrate concentration of each sample was determined before the study began and in cortical bone it was found to be remarkably uniform, averaging 1.96 ± 0.06 weight%. The citrate concentration decreased with regularity in a series of samples which were buried, but in samples which were stored in a laboratory setting for an extended period of time, there was no loss of citrate. The authors speculated that soil organisms and moisture were required to allow citrate to be consumed. A regression model was formulated which accounted for the regular loss of citrate concentration with time and with which, by extrapolation, the citrate concentration was expected to reach zero concentration in about 95 years. Within broad limits the storage conditions of temperature, humidity, and depth of burial did not influence the rate of loss although the study suggested that no citrate loss occurred when the samples had not been exposed to moist soil and there was no loss of citrate at temperatures below $0°C$. A mathematical formula was developed relating the rate of citrate decrease to the PMI for ground-surface-deposited bones. Schwarcz et al. (2010) concluded that the citrate content of bone could be used to estimate the PMI up to a limit of 100 years with a minimum error of 1% of the age of the bone specimen, but further testing of the method with samples contrasted with control samples of known PMI and uniform storage conditions was required.

A recent study was conducted by Kanz and colleagues (2014) to examine the accuracy of the model proposed by Schwarcz and colleagues and to identify potential differences in the citrate degradation process. Twenty bodies which were buried in a cemetery, over the period from 1948 to 1973, were exhumed because the cemetery was being abandoned. There were equal numbers of each sex and the ages and the PMIs of each body were known. Half of the bodies were buried in wooden coffins and half were also in wooden coffins but with the addition of plastic body bags with degradable backs, in order to contain escaped gases while the bodies were in the mortuary. The bodies had been buried to a depth of $1.4-3.0$ m and were exhumed at the same time but the length of burial varied between 52 and 27 years. All bodies had largely decomposed and had been in contact with soil when exhumed. After removal the bodies were stored in dry conditions at a controlled temperature for 10 years before skeletal analysis for citrate concentration was carried out. Kantz and colleagues postulated that because the loss of citrate depended on the action of moisture and soil organisms, the concentration would have remained stable during the 10-year period of storage in dry conditions. The citrate concentration was then determined in two types of bone: from the temporal bone and from the mid-shaft of the femur.

The results of the analysis of the temporal bones revealed that the PMI was underestimated in the group buried without body bags by about 19.2 years and overestimated in those buried in body bags by 5.2 years. This difference was statistically significant. When the femoral bones were analyzed, no significant difference was found between the two groups but there was an underestimation of about 16.3 years in those buried without body bags and a slight overestimation of 0.4 years in the body bag group. When the results were tested with the model developed by Schwarcz and colleagues, the accuracy was low. In discussing the results, the authors suggested that the underestimation of the PMI in the bodies buried without body bags contradicted the hypothesis that there needed to be direct contact of bone, after decomposition, with moisture for the process of citrate degradation, further postulating that the disintegration of the decomposable back panels of the plastic body bags allowed the soil and humidity to enter the body bags and start the process of citrate degradation which might even be accelerated by the enclosing nature of the surrounding plastic keeping the soil humidity high. When femoral bone was used for citrate analysis, despite there being no significant difference in citrate decomposition rates between the two buried groups, decomposition was slightly faster in the body bag group because of the accelerant effect of the body bags. Decomposition was also slower with femoral bone compared with temporal bone. It was recommended therefore that bone with a thick outer cortex be used in citrate analysis and such bone might facilitate the estimation of the PMI for longer periods into the past. Because citrate degradation was slower in buried bones than surface-deposited bones, different mathematical models might require to be calculated for bones deposited in different environments and also for the different types of bones analyzed.

Kanz and colleagues concluded that citrate-based PMI determination had promising potential for use in forensic cases but that at present, concentrations of citrate above 0.140 weight% in well-preserved bones might be taken as an indication that the bones were less than 50 years old in soil-buried remains.

Raman Spectroscopy

A novel approach to the chemical investigation of buried bone as a method of determining the PMI was recently investigated by McLaughlin and Lednev (2011). Raman spectroscopy uses laser light directed on to a sample. Small portions of photons are scattered which have a different energy than the light source. A Raman spectrum is obtained by detecting these inelastically scattered photons. The energy difference, or Raman shift, between the laser source and the scattered photons corresponds to molecular vibrational models, with different molecules producing different vibrations. A Raman spectrum can therefore be used to give information about the identity, structure, and properties of various materials based on their vibrational transitions.

Fragments of a turkey leg bone, after removal of all flesh, were buried in soil and a different fragment removed and examined spectroscopically at 2-week intervals up to 68 days. These fragments were compared with a fragment which had not been buried and a fragment treated with collagenase solution. During burial there was a gradual loss of the mineral phase of the bone, exposing the collagen phase to hydrolysis. It was found that as burial time increased the Raman spectrum of certain collagenous organic molecules decreased. This was not seen with unburied bone but there were similarities between the buried bone samples and the collagenase-treated sample. McLaughlin and Lednev in commenting on these promising results suggested research should be continued to develop a Raman spectroscopic model to extrapolate bone burial duration and which factored in the variables of soil pH, burial temperature, humidity, and the presence of soft tissue. The study should also be extended to ascertain whether the observed trends continued with longer burial time.

Carbon Dating and the Use of Naturally Occurring and Artificial Radioactive Isotopes

Radioactive isotopes occur naturally in every environment and can also be produced artificially. The type and concentration of natural radioactive isotopes such as radon (^{226}Ra), polonium (^{210}Po), lead (^{210}Pb), uranium (^{238}U, ^{235}U, ^{232}U), and thorium (^{232}Th) have a regular, predictable background concentration which has remained unchanged for thousands of years and which have been shown not to produce identifiable increases when ingested into the body in industrial environments where they are more prevalent (Smith et al., 2001). The commonest natural radioisotope is Carbon 14 (^{14}C), which becomes rapidly oxidized in the atmosphere to form radioactive carbon dioxide (^{14}CO$_2$). It enters the food chain by the processes of solution in the oceans and photosynthesis in plants. It becomes incorporated in bone through dietary ingestion of plant and animal material and its rate of decay can be measured to give an estimate of the age of ancient bones up to 50,000 years BP (Knight and Lauder, 1969), although estimating age as old as this was later disputed (Van der Plicht, 2004). Anderson and colleagues (1947) detected and identified ^{14}C. They later calculated the half-life of ^{14}C to be 5720 ± 47 years but made the false assumption that radiocarbon in the environment had remained constant over millions of years so that modern values could be correlated to initial concentrations in historical materials (Libby et al., 1949). Subsequently it was found that ^{14}C does not decay in a regular manner; a radiocarbon age is not equivalent to a calendar age as fluctuations of atmospheric ^{14}C concentration, known as the de Vries effects, have occurred throughout the centuries (Taylor et al., 1989). A large fluctuation of ^{14}C occurred in the period 11,000−14,500 BP due to changes in the production rate, caused by geomagnetic and solar modulation of the cosmic-ray flux and the carbon cycle, although it has also been suggested that the fluctuation was due to carbon cycle changes tied to deep ocean currents (Fairbanks et al., 2005). Hence, a calibration is required, which, to be accurate and precise, should ideally be based on an absolutely dated record that has carbon incorporated directly from the atmosphere at the time of formation.

In the recent past, two major fluctuations in ^{14}C levels have been documented for the years 1900−1982, both of which had an anthropogenic cause (Taylor et al., 1989). After the onset of the Industrial Revolution, burning of fossil fuel increased and because it was millions of years old the ^{14}C in fossil fuel had almost completely decayed. As a result the ^{14}C in the biosphere became diluted by the non-radioactive isotopes of carbon. This was particularly noted in the period 1910−50 when the amount of ^{14}C in the environment decreased on average by 3%. This fluctuation is known as the *Suess* or *fossil fuel effect* (Taylor et al., 1989). From about 1950 there was a large increase of ^{14}C in the atmosphere as a result of nuclear weapons testing. This entered the biosphere and was eventually incorporated in bone. Atmospheric nuclear testing ceased in 1963, but the atmospheric ^{14}C did not drop to pre-1950 levels until about the mid-1990s. This second recent fluctuation is known as the *Libby* or *bomb effect* (Taylor et al., 1989). Attempts were made to correct the de Vries effects, which were prevalent before the anthropogenic effects of the 20th century and the anomalies produced by 20th century fossil fuels and nuclear testing, by correlating ^{14}C levels in the environment with ^{14}C in tree rings of known age from around the world. Three categories of classifying ^{14}C in bone material were proposed by Taylor et al. (1989):

1. Nonmodern before AD 1650.
2. Premodern from AD 1650 to 1950.
3. Modern from AD 1950 to the present time.

However, the error rate in the second category was ± 300 years. Since the work of Taylor and colleagues (1989), attempts have continued to better estimate the date of material by producing corrective calibration curves for the various geographical areas. The ^{14}C in the atmosphere is incorporated into the annual growth ring of any nearby tree. Although it is rare to find trees older than about 12,000 years BP, analysis of ^{14}C in marine corals, foraminifera, plant macrofossils, and speleothems both in the northern and southern hemispheres, can enable estimation of the age of bones and other material by radiocarbon dating to be extended before this time period (Fairbanks et al., 2005). At the present time new calibration curves are produced every few years as new material becomes available. With the present calibration curve, devised in 2013, it is possible to date material as far back as 50,000 years BP (Reimer et al., 2013). The advent of accelerated mass spectrometry has also made it easier to carbon date, as much smaller quantities of material can be used and the measurement time has been reduced from weeks to minutes (Fairbanks et al., 2005). When radiocarbon dating is reported in "years BP", BP (Before Present) refers to the number of years before 1950, the beginning of nuclear weapons testing (Ubelaker, 2014). In recent times since the period of elevated atmospheric ^{14}C resulting from nuclear weapons testing, it has been found that the incorporation of ^{14}C into the different body tissues and its elimination from them varies greatly depending on the turnover rate, making its use in forensic cases difficult (Ubelaker, 2014). Ubelaker and others have shown that by using the known elevation of ^{14}C in various body tissues at different time periods during the increased levels which occurred from 1963 to the mid-1990s, it may be of some use in recent forensic cases (Ubelaker, 2014; Wild et al., 2000; Ubelaker and Parra, 2011; Ubelaker et al., 2015).

Artificial radioactive isotopes, which have greatly increased in the natural environment since nuclear testing began in 1945, have been investigated as a means of estimating the PMI because they are less affected by changes within the physical environment to which the bones have been exposed than are methods which depend on chemical changes (Swift, 2006). Maclaughlin-Black and colleagues (1992) investigated the use of Strontium-90 (^{90}Sr) in order to distinguish modern bone from bone deposited before nuclear testing began. Strontium and calcium, both alkaline earth metals, have a similar structure but, unlike calcium, which is an essential mammalian nutrient and is incorporated in bone, strontium has no known metabolic function. Strontium is not incorporated in the body unless calcium is deficient and then only in a lesser concentration than calcium. Both are taken up in the body by absorption through the intestine and incorporated in the hydroxyapatite matrix of bone. ^{90}Sr, the radioactive isotope of strontium, greatly increased in the atmosphere after nuclear testing began in 1945, became distributed worldwide, and reached a peak in the early 1960s. It was eventually taken up by vegetation, entered the food chain, and gradually became incorporated in human bone. It was suggested that if a date could be defined when ^{90}Sr entered the food chain, people who died before that date should not possess detectable levels of ^{90}Sr in their bones, whereas people dying after that date would have detectable levels. ^{90}Sr levels were measured in three medieval femora and compared with levels in three modern postmortem femora (Maclaughlin-Black et al., 1992). A significantly higher level of ^{90}Sr was found in the modern bones compared with the medieval bones, but a small amount of ^{90}Sr still present in the medieval bones was attributed to diagenesis which the authors defined as the postmortem exchange of chemicals between the skeleton and its surrounding medium. Laboratory contamination of archeological specimens and possible contamination from surrounding soil was not accounted for in this study and Maclaughlin-Black and colleagues admitted that a larger study was required to confirm the findings. They concluded that it was possible that the increased concentration of ^{90}Sr in the atmosphere since the 1960s and its incorporation in the diet was the reason for its increased concentration in the modern bone samples. The method might prove to be of some value in determining whether an individual was alive before or after the time period when artificial radionuclides were introduced into the food chain.

In a similar study, ^{90}Sr levels in nine samples of occipital bone from skulls, three from the years 1931 and 1932, and the rest from the years 1989 to 1994 were analyzed by Neis and colleagues (1999). All the samples were from bodies autopsied in a university forensic pathology department and none had been buried. There was no significant concentration of ^{90}Sr in three samples of bone from 1931/32, before nuclear testing began. However, none of these samples had been subjected to soil diagenesis. In the group of six samples from 1989 to 1994, a single sample exhibited a small concentration of ^{90}Sr, explained by the fact that skeletal growth had already been completed before the nuclear fallout. Another group of two samples with a moderate concentration of ^{90}Sr was due to skeletal growth not being completed before the fallout and the last group of three samples had a high concentration of ^{90}Sr because the dates of birth occurred during the fallout. This was a study of a small number of samples, none of which had been buried and the authors suggested that the major problem was to determine the cut-off year for measurable ^{90}Sr in skeletal remains, taking into consideration that the biological half-life of ^{90}Sr was 7.5−18 years and the physical half-life was 28.1 years. Another problem concerned the estimation of ^{90}Sr in buried bodies. Most bodies were buried between 1 and 5 m below the surface, ^{90}Sr activity could never reach more than 80 cm below the surface and its rate of penetration was only 1 cm per year.

Swift (1998) investigated the use of naturally occurring radioactive polonium (^{210}Po) and radioactive lead (^{210}Pb), both part of the radon (^{226}Ra) series, for their usefulness in estimating the PMI. ^{210}Po is a decay product of ^{210}Pb and neither is produced by nuclear explosions. They are mainly inhaled and ingested from food and although 10−15% of ^{210}Pb is incorporated in bone in a few hours, uptake is slow. Eventually 90% of all lead found in the body is incorporated in bone. ^{210}Po has a half-life of 138.4 days and the half-life of ^{210}Pb is 22.3 years. The ratio between the two in life is in equilibrium but after death it alters as the two isotopes decay in an exponential manner and this, theoretically, should allow a predictable PMI to be calculated from the altering ratio by reference back to the known ratio in life. Swift tested various bone samples for ^{210}Po and ^{210}Pb and concluded that the ratio between the two was readily measurable, allowing quantities to be ascertained accurately. ^{210}Pb was also abundant naturally and given its half-life of 22.3 years, would be a useful radioisotope for forensic use. One disadvantage was that shellfish consumption and smoking were known to affect ^{210}Pb levels. Other disadvantages were the expense of analysis, possible variation in different parts of the skeleton, individual variation in lead metabolism, and the effects of diagenesis. Swift suggested a larger study of ancient and modern bones in which the time of death was known, together with the testing of soil samples to gauge the effects of diagenesis, in order to determine the usefulness of the estimation of ^{210}Pb in bone.

A number of radioisotopes as well as trace elements were investigated for their potential use as indicators of PMI by Swift and colleagues (2001) in a pilot study. The authors listed the requirements of a radioisotope if it was to be of forensic use as:

1. To have a half-life commensurate with the time scale of investigation, that is, less than 40 years.
2. To be abundant enough to be detected by conventional analytical techniques.
3. To have some biological function so as to be incorporated in human bone.

Fifteen samples of skeletal material exhumed from soil burials in a Portuguese cemetery, with PMIs ranging from 15 to 77 years, were treated and analyzed for various radionuclides. There was a correlation between the PMI and concentrations of ^{238}U, ^{234}U, ^{210}Po, and ^{210}Pb from the Uranium series as well as with the non-natural radionuclides ^{238}Pu, ^{239}Pu, ^{240}Pu (Plutonium), and ^{137}Cs (Cesium). Trace element analysis revealed intercorrelations as well as correlations with the TSD. Swift concluded that these radionuclides and trace elements could be used to give some quantitative data regarding the postmortem interment period but further studies were required to create a population-specific calibration scale, given the variation in isotope exposures in different countries with different geologic strata and different diets.

At the present time the status of estimation of the PMI by the use of naturally occurring radioisotopes and trace elements has mainly been of importance in distinguishing archeological from forensic material, but the recent work by Ubelaker may extend its usefulness to remains of more recent forensic interest (Ubelaker, 2014; Ubelaker and Parra, 2011). Future research will depend on the influence of soil characteristics in different soil types, the leaching by exposure of bones to water, the comparison of radioisotope concentration in different bone types, and the effect of diet and other lifestyle influences on radioisotope uptake in bone (Howard, 2008).

CONCLUSIONS

In the latter stages of decomposition, factors such as burial environment and insect activity play a major role in the nature and speed of decomposition. One of the key variables in decomposition, temperature, will be modified by soil and water (eg, sea, lake, river) contexts, and decomposition will tend (depending on season) to be faster above the surface than below. Particular burial contexts can also significantly delay the rate of decomposition through natural processes of mummification or saponification. Insects have a major role in determining the rate of decomposition and their activity will also be regulated by temperature. While the use of insects in forensic contexts has a long history, the study of insect life cycles and carcass colonization successions only developed into the science of forensic entomology in the 20th century. It is often the chief tool for estimating the TSD in the post-48-hour postmortem period. Considering the estimation of the PMI in skeletonized remains, a range of methods, for the most part dictated by context, are available. Some of the methods reviewed include examination of associated botanical remains, assessment of residual soft tissues, histological examination of bone degradation, physicochemical changes to bone (with the citrate concentration in bone having some potential value in estimating the PMI), as well as radioactive isotope concentrations. However, the error ranges for the majority of these approaches are uncomfortably large.

REFERENCES

Adlam, R.E., Simmons, T., 2007. The effect of repeated physical disturbance on soft tissue decomposition – are taphonomic studies an accurate reflection of decomposition? J. Forensic Sci. 52 (5), 1007–1014.

Amendt, J., et al., 2007. Best practice in forensic entomology – standards and guidelines. Int. J. Legal Med. 121, 90–104.

Amy, R., et al., 1986. The last Franklin expedition: report of a post-mortem examination of a crew member. Can. Med. Assoc. J. 135, 115–117.

Anderson, E.C., Libby, W.F., et al., 1947. Natural radiocarbon from cosmic radiation. Phys. Rev. 72 (10), 931–936.

Anderson, G.S., 2000. Minimum and maximum development rates of some forensically important Calliphoridae (Diptera). J. Forensic Sci. 45 (4), 824–832.

Anderson, G.S., 2011. Comparison of decomposition rates and faunal colonization of carrion in indoor and outdoor environments. J. Forensic Sci. 56 (1), 136–142.

Anderson, G.S., Van Laerhoven, S.L., 1996. Initial studies on insect succession on carrion in south western British Columbia. J. Forensic Sci. 41 (4), 617–625.

Archer, M.S., 2004. The effect of time after body discovery on the accuracy of retrospective weather station ambient temperature corrections in forensic entomology. J. Forensic Sci. 49 (3), 1–7.

Archer, M.S., Elgar, M.A., 2003. Yearly activity patterns in southern Victoria (Australia) of seasonally active carrion insects. Forensic Sci. Int. 132, 173–176.

Arnold, C.Y., 1959. The determination and significance of the base temperature in a linear heat system. Proc. Am. Soc. Hortic. Sci. 74, 430–445.

Aufderheide, A.C., 1981. Soft tissue paleopathology – an emerging specialty. Hum. Pathol. 12 (10), 865–867.

Bachmann, M.D., Simmons, T., 2010. The influence of pre-burial insect access on the decomposition rate. J. Forensic Sci. 55 (4), 893–900.

Behrensmeyer, A.K., 1978. Taphonomic and ecologic information from bone weathering. Paleobiology 4 (2), 150–162.

Bell, L.S., Skinner, M.F., Jones, S.J., 1996. The speed of post-mortem change to the human skeleton and its taphonomic significance. Forensic Sci. Int. 82, 129–140.

Benecke, M., 2001. A brief history of forensic entomology. Forensic Sci. Int. 120, 2–14.

Breitmeir, D., et al., 2005. Evaluation of the correlation between time corpses spent in – ground graves and findings at exhumation. Forensic Sci. Int. 154, 218–233.

Campobasso, C.P., Di Vella, G., Introna, F., 2001. Factors affecting decomposition and Diptera colonisation. Forensic Sci. Int. 120, 18–27.

Carter, D.O., Yellowlees, D., Tibbett, M., 2010. Moisture can be the dominant environmental parameter governing cadaver decomposition in soil. Forensic Sci. Int. 200, 60–66.

Cattaneo, C., Gelsthorpe, K., Phillips, P., Sokol, R.J., 1992. Reliable identification of human albumin in ancient bone using ELISA and monoclonal antibodies. Am. J. Phys. Anthropol. 87, 365–372.

Courtin, G.M., Fairgrieve, S.I., 2004. Evaluation of post-mortem interval (PMI) as revealed through the analysis of annual growth in woody tissue. J. Forensic Sci. 49 (4), 1–3.

Dent, B.B., Forbes, S.L., Stuart, B.H., 2004. Review of human decomposition processes in soil. Environ. Geol. 45 (4), 576–585.

Edwards, R., Chaney, W., Bergman, M., 1987. Temperature developmental units for insects. Pest Crop Newslett. Purdue Univ. 2, 5–6.

Facchini, F., Pettener, D., 1977. Chemical and physical methods in dating human skeletal remains. Am. J. Phys. Anthropol. 47, 65–70.

Fairbanks, R.G., et al., 2005. Radiocarbon calibration curve spanning 0 to 50,000 years BP based on paired ^{230}Th/^{234}U/^{238}U and ^{14}C dates on pristine corals. Quat. Sci. Rev. 24, 1781–1796.

Forbes, S.L., 2008. Forensic chemistry: applications to decomposition and preservation. In: Oxenham, M. (Ed.), Approaches to Death, Disaster and Abuse. Australian Academic Press, Brisbane, Ch. 15.

Forbes, S.L., Stuart, B.H., Dadour, I., Dent, B.B., 2004. A preliminary investigation of the stages of adipocere formation. J. Forensic Sci. 49 (3), 1–9.

Forbes, S.L., Stuart, B.H., Dent, B.B., 2005. The effect of the burial environment on adipocere formation. Forensic Sci. Int. 154, 24–34.

Galloway, A., et al., 1989. Decay rates of human remains in an arid environment. J. Forensic Sci. 34 (3), 607–616.

Gill-King, H., 1997. Chemical and ultrastructural aspects of decomposition. In: Haglund, W.D., Sorg, M.H. (Eds.), Forensic Taphonomy: The Post Mortem Fate of Human Remains. CRC Press, Boca Raton, pp. 93–108.

Goff, M.L., 1991. Comparison of insect species associated with decomposing remains recovered inside dwellings and outdoors on the Island of Oahu, Hawaii. J. Forensic Sci. 36, 748–753.

Goff, M.L., 1993. Estimation of post-mortem interval using arthropod development and successional patterns. Forensic Sci. Rev. 5 (2), 82–94.

Goff, M.L., Flynn, M.M., 1991. Determination of post-mortem interval by arthropod succession: a case study from the Hawaiian Islands. J. Forensic Sci. 36 (2), 607–614.

Gotouda, H., et al., 1988. The Mechanism of experimental adipocere formation: hydration and dehydrogenation in microbial synthesis of hydroxy and oxo fatty acids. Forensic Sci. Int. 37, 249–257.

Grassberger, M., Reiter, C., 2001. Effect of temperature on *Lucilia sericata* (Diptera: Calliphoridae) development with special reference to the isomegalen- and isomorphen- diagram. Forensic Sci. Int. 120, 32–36.

Harvey, M.L., Mansell, M.W., Villet, M.H., Dadour, I.R., 2003. Molecular identification of some forensically important blowflies of southern Africa and Australia. Med. Vet. Entomol. 17, 363–369.

Hedges, R.E.M., 2002. Bone diagenesis: an overview of processes. Archaeometry 44, 319–328.

Hoke, N., et al., 2011. Estimating the chance of success of archaeometric analyses of bone: UV induced bone fluorescence compared to histological screening. Paleogeogr. Paleoclimatol. Paleoecol. 310, 23–31.

Hoke, N., Grigat, A., Grupe, G., Harbeck, M., 2013. Reconsideration of bone post-mortem interval estimation by UV-induced auto fluorescence. Forensic Sci. Int. 228, 176e1–176e6.

Howard, S., 2008. A Preliminary Investigation into the Estimation of Time since Death from Human Skeletal Remains by Radioisotope and Trace Element Analysis. Master of Forensic Science Thesis. University of Western Australia.

Introna, F., Di Vella, G., Campobasso, C.P., 1999. Determination of post-mortem interval from old skeletal remains by image analysis of luminol test results. J. Forensic Sci. 44 (3), 535–538.

Jarvis, D.R., 1997. Nitrogen levels in long bones from coffin burials interred for periods of 26–90 years. Forensic Sci. Int. 85, 199–208.

Johnson, A.P., Wallman, J.F., Archer, M.S., 2012. Experimental and casework validation of ambient temperature corrections in forensic entomology. J. Forensic Sci. 57 (1), 215–221.

Kanz, F., Reiter, C., Risser, D., 2014. Citrate content of bone for time since death estimation: results from burials with different characteristics and known PMI. J. Forensic Sci. 59 (3), 613–620.

Knight, B., Lauder, I., 1967. Practical methods of dating skeletal remains: a preliminary study. Med. Sci. Law 7, 205–209.

Knight, B., Lauder, I., 1969. Methods of dating skeletal remains. Hum. Biol. 41 (3), 322–341.

Komar, D.A., 1998. Decay rates in a cold climate region: a review of cases involving advanced decomposition from the Medical Examiner's Office in Edmonton, Alberta. J. Forensic Sci. 43 (1), 57–61.

Libby, W.F., Anderson, E.C., Arnold, J.R., 1949. Age determination by radiocarbon content: worldwide assay of natural radiocarbon. Science 109 (2827), 227–228.

Lowenstein, J.M., 1981. Immunological reactions from fossil material. Philos. Trans. R. Soc. Lond. B 292, 143–149.

Maclaughlin-Black, S.M., et al., 1992. Strontium-90 as an indicator of time since death: a pilot investigation. Forensic Sci. Int. 57, 51–56.

Mann, R.W., Bass, W.M., Meadows, L., 1990. Time since death and decomposition of the human body: variables and observations in case and experimental field studies. J. Forensic Sci. 35 (1), 103–111.

Matuszewski, S., et al., 2008. An initial study of insect succession and carrion decomposition in various forest habitats of Central Europe. Forensic Sci. Int. 180, 61–69.

Matuszewski, S., et al., 2010a. Insect succession and carrion decomposition in selected forests of Central Europe. Part I: pattern and rate of decomposition. Forensic Sci. Int. 194, 85–93.

Matuszewski, S., et al., 2010b. Insect succession and carrion decomposition in selected forests of Central Europe. Part II: composition and residency patterns of carrion fauna. Forensic Sci. Int. 195, 42–51.

McLaughlin, G., Lednev, I.K., 2011. Potential application of Raman spectroscopy for determining burial duration of skeletal remains. Anal. Bioanal. Chem. 401, 2511–2518.

Neis, P., et al., 1999. Strontium 90 for determination of time since death. Forensic Sci. Int. 99, 47–51.

Notter, S.J., Stuart, B.H., Rowe, R., Langlois, N., 2009. The initial changes of fat deposits during the decomposition of human and pig remains. J. Forensic Sci. 54 (1), 195–201.

O'Brien, T.G., Kuehner, A.C., 2007. Waxing grave about adipocere: soft tissue change in an aquatic environment. J. Forensic Sci. 52 (2), 294–301.

Payne, J.A., 1965. A summer carrion study of the baby pig Sus scrofa Linnaeus. Ecology 46 (5), 592–602.

Perper, J.A., 2006. Time of death and changes after death. In: Spitz, W.U. (Ed.), Spitz and Fisher's Medico Legal Investigation of Death, fourth ed. Charles C Springer, Springfield, Illinois, pp. 107–108. Ch. 3.

Pohjoismäki, J.L.O., et al., 2010. Indoors forensic entomology: colonisation of human remains in closed environments by specific species of sarcophagous flies. Forensic Sci. Int. 199, 38–42.

Prieto, J.L., Magaña, C., Ubelaker, D.H., 2004. Interpretation of post-mortem change in cadavers in Spain. J. Forensic Sci. 49 (5), 1–6.

Ramsthaler, F., Kreutz, K., Zipp, K., Verhoff, M.A., 2009. Dating skeletal remains with luminol-chemiluminescence. Validity, intra- and interobserver error. Forensic Sci. Int. 187, 47–50.

Ramsthaler, F., Ebach, S.C., Birngruber, C.G., Verhoff, M.A., 2011. Post-mortem interval of skeletal remains through the detection of intraosseal haemin traces. A comparison of UV-fluorescence, luminol, Hexagon-OBTI® and Combur® tests. Forensic Sci. Int. 209, 59–63.

Réaumur, R.A.F., 1735. Observations du thérmomètre faites à Paris pendant l'année 1735, comparées avec celles qui ont été faites sous la ligne; à l'Isle de France, à Alger et en quelques-unes de nos Isles de l'Amérique. Mémoires de l'Académie des Sciences 545–576.

Reeves, N.M., 2009. Taphonomic effects of vulture scavenging. J. Forensic Sci. 54 (3), 523–528.

Reimer, P.J., et al., 2013. INTCAL13 and Marine 13 radiocarbon age calibration curves 0-50,000 years cal BP. Radiocarbon 55 (4), 1869–1887.

Rivers, D.B., Thompson, C., Brogan, R., 2011. Physiological trade-offs of forming maggot masses by necrophagous flies on vertebrate carrion. Bull. Entomol. Res. 101, 599–611.

Rodriguez, W.C., Bass, W.M., 1983. Insect activity and its relationship to decay rates of human cadavers in East Tennessee. J. Forensic Sci. 28 (2), 423–432.

Rodriguez, W.C., Bass, W.M., 1985. Decomposition of buried bodies and methods that may aid in their location. J. Forensic Sci. 30 (3), 836–852.

Schultz, M., 1997. Microscopic investigation of excavated skeletal remains: a contribution to palaeopathology and forensic medicine. In: Haglund, W.D., Sorg, M.H. (Eds.), Forensic Taphonomy: The Postmortem Fate of Human Remains. CRC Press, Boca Raton, Ch. 14.

Schwarcz, H.P., Agur, K., Jantz, L.M., 2010. A new method for determination of post-mortem interval: citrate content of bone. J. Forensic Sci. 55 (6), 1516–1522.

Simmons, T., et al., 2010a. The influence of insects on decomposition rate in buried and surface remains. J. Forensic Sci. 55 (4), 889–892.

Simmons, T., Adlam, R.E., Moffatt, C., 2010b. Debugging decomposition data – comparative taphonomic studies and the influence of insects and carcass size and decomposition rate. J. Forensic Sci. 55 (1), 8–13.

Sledzik, P.S., Micozzi, M.S., 1997. Autopsied, embalmed and preserved human remains: distinguishing features in forensic and historic contexts. In: Haglund, W.D., Sorg, M.H. (Eds.), Forensic Taphonomy: The Post-mortem Fate of Human Remains. CRC Press, Boca Raton, FL, pp. 483–495.

Smith, K.R., et al., 2001. The Radiological Impact of Coal-Fired Electricity Generation in the UK. NRPB-R327, National Radiological Protection Board Report.

Spradley, M.K., Hamilton, M.D., Giordano, A., 2012. Spatial patterning of vulture scavenged human remains. Forensic Sci. Int. 219, 57–63.

Steadman, D.W., Worne, H., 2007. Canine scavenging of human remains in an indoor setting. Forensic Sci. Int. 173, 78–82.

Sung Tz'u, 1186–1249. The Washing Away of Wrongs. Translated from the Chinese by McKnight, B.E., 1981. University of Michigan, Ann Arbor, pp. 69–70.

Swift, B., 1998. Dating human skeletal remains: investigating the viability of measuring the equilibrium between ^{210}Po and ^{210}Pb as a means of estimating the post-mortem interval. Forensic Sci. Int. 98, 119–126.

Swift, B., 2006. The timing of death. In: Rutty, G. (Ed.), Essentials of Autopsy Practice. Springer-Verlag, London, Ch. 8.

Swift, B., Lauder, I., Black, S., Norris, J., 2001. An estimation of the post-mortem interval in human skeletal remains: a radionuclide and trace element approach. Forensic Sci. Int. 117, 73–87.

Taylor, R.E., Suchey, J.M., Payen, L.A., Slota, P.J., 1989. The use of radiocarbon (^{14}C) to identify human skeletal materials of forensic scientific interest. J. Forensic Sci. 34 (5), 1196–1205.

Ubelaker, D.H., 2014. Radiocarbon analysis of human remains: a review of forensic applications. J. Forensic Sci. 59 (6), 1466–1472.

Ubelaker, D.H., Parra, R.C., 2011. Radiocarbon analysis of dental enamel and bone to evaluate date of birth and death: perspective from the southern hemisphere. Forensic Sci. Int. 208, 103–107.

Ubelaker, D.H., Zarenko, K.M., 2011. Adipocere: what is known after two centuries of research. Forensic Sci. Int. 208, 167–172.

Ubelaker, D.H., Thomas, C., Olson, J.E., 2015. The impact of age at death on the lag time of radiocarbon values in human bone. Forensic Sci. Int. 251, 56–60.

Van der Plicht, J., 2004. Radiocarbon calibration – past, present and future. Nucl. Instrum. Methods Phys. Res. B 223–224, 353–358.

Vass, A.A., et al., 1992. Time since death determinations in human cadavers using soil solution. J. Forensic Sci. 37 (5), 1236–1253.

Wallman, J.F., 2001. A key to the adults of species of blowflies in southern Australia known or suspected to breed in carrion. Med. Vet. Entomol. 15, 433–437.

Wallman, J.F., 2002. Winged evidence: forensic identification of blowflies. Aust. J. Forensic Sci. 34 (2), 73–79.

Wallman, J.F., Leys, R., Hogendoorn, K., 2005. Molecular systematics of Australian carrion-breeding blowflies (Diptera: Calliphoridae) based on mitochondrial DNA. Invertebr. Syst. 19, 1–15.

Wang, J.Y., 1960. A critique of the heat unit approach to plant response studies. Ecology 41 (4), 785–790.

White, L., Booth, T.J., 2014. The origin of bacteria responsible for bio erosion to the internal microstructure: results from experimentally deposited pig carcasses. Forensic Sci. Int. 239, 92–102.

White, E.M., Hannus, L.A., 1983. Chemical weathering of bone in archaeological soils. Am. Antiq. 48 (2), 316–322.

Wild, E.M., et al., 2000. ^{14}C dating with the bomb peak: and application to forensic medicine. Nucl. Instrum. Methods Phys. Res. B 172, 944–950.

Willey, P., Heilman, A., 1987. Estimating time since death using plant roots and stems. J. Forensic Sci. 32 (5), 1264–1270.

Wilson, A.S., et al., 2007. Modelling the buried human body environment in upland climes using three contrasting field sites. Forensic Sci. Int. 169, 6–18.

Yan, F., McNally, R., Kontanis, E.J., Sadik, O.A., 2001. Preliminary quantitative investigation of post-mortem adipocere formation. J. Forensic Sci. 46 (3), 609–614.

Yoshino, M., et al., 1991. Microscopical study on estimation of time since death in skeletal remains. Forensic Sci. Int. 49, 143–158.

CHAPTER 5

Recent Research and Current Trends

In the mid-13th century Sung Tz'u (see chapters: Supravital Reactions in the Estimation of the Time Since Death (TSD) and Research in the Later Stages of Decomposition) elaborated on the variable nature and rate of decomposition in the four seasons. In concluding this section in his handbook, which includes some detailed descriptions of the decomposition process, he notes, "In extremely cold weather, five days is equivalent to one day in a time of great heat, and half a month the equivalent of three or four extremely hot days" (Sung Tz'u, 1186–1249).

Not a great deal has changed over the intervening 700 plus years with, until recently, most studies into autolysis and putrefaction continuing to be of a descriptive and qualitative nature, describing the various stages, the factors involved, the biochemistry of the process and other factors affecting it. Only in the last decade has it been recognized that, if advances are to be made in the estimation of the postmortem interval (PMI), quantification of the process is required. In their review paper on the estimation of the PMI, Henssge and Madea (2007) state that the main principle of determination of the time since death (TSD) should be:

> the calculation of a measurable date along a time dependent curve back to the start point" and that, "most methods proposed for estimation of the time

Human Body Decomposition. DOI: http://dx.doi.org/10.1016/B978-0-12-803691-4.00010-8

since death are of only academic interest since they describe just post-mortem changes. They only gain practical relevance if the following criteria are fulfilled: quantitative measurement, mathematical description, taking into account influencing factors quantitatively, declaration of precision and proof of precision on independent material.

Henssge and Madea (2007, p. 183)

Two main approaches to quantifying decomposition in the later stages have evolved in recent years: firstly, how to determine a mathematical scale of the decomposition process, and secondly, how to determine a model which incorporates the decomposition process with the main variables affecting decomposition, namely, temperature, insect access, burial depth, humidity, trauma, body size and weight, the presence or absence of clothing, and random and opportune animal scavenging.

DEVELOPMENT OF A GRADING SYSTEM OF HUMAN DECOMPOSITION

Attempts to quantify the stages of decomposition were first made by entomologists studying insect successions colonizing carrion during decomposition. Reed (1958) studied insect species successions on 43 dog carcasses in a variety of environments while they decomposed. He recognized four stages—fresh, bloated, decay, and dry—and he quoted previous authors who had staged the decomposition process: Mégnin (1894), who recognized eight stages; Fuller (1934), who recognized three stages; and Howden (1950), who recognized two stages. These were early classifications of the stages of decomposition.

In a seminal study, Payne (1965) researched decomposition in animals with and without insect access. He found that decomposition in small animals such as frogs, toads, mice, shrews, rats, and chipmunks was too rapid to allow the detailed study of insect succession and the feathers in chickens caused problems in recognition and estimation of insects. He found baby pigs more suitable for the study. Recognizing decomposition as a continuous process, he described in detail six stages of decomposition: fresh, bloated, active decay, advanced decay, dry, and remains. He found a defined insect succession at each stage of decomposition and that carcasses exposed to insects decomposed more rapidly.

governing the release of VFA production. Temperature was recorded from readings obtained from the nearest national weather station and adjusted with a corrective factor obtained by recording daily temperatures, taken for a week at the site of the decomposing cadavers. If the temperature fell below 4°C it became much more difficult to estimate the TSD from a single time point as the decomposition process slowed and any temperature below 0°C was regarded as being 0°C. It took 1285 ± 110 ADDs for a body to become skeletonized or for VFA production to fall below detectable limits. This enabled a graph to be constructed in which TSD was plotted against temperature, thus providing a rough estimate of the TSD (Fig. 5.1). The emphasis in this study was to estimate the PMI from the concentration of VFAs and to correlate this with ADDs rather than with the stage of decomposition.

Later, Vass and colleagues (2002) also studied 18 bodies over a 4-year period with the purpose of identifying chemical biomarkers in the heart, lung, brain, kidney, liver, and muscle associated with early decomposition. The authors quoted the reported accuracy of the estimation of VFAs as a method of estimating the TSD as being ± 2 days in preskeletonized bodies and ± 2 weeks in skeletonized bodies. It was suggested that if the rate of breakdown in decomposition of the large biomolecules of proteins, nucleic acids, lipids, and polysaccharides into their smaller component molecules could be measured, the rate might

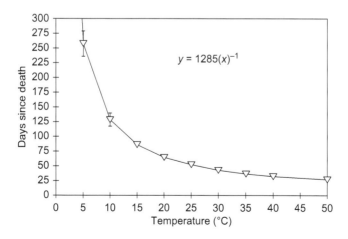

Figure 5.1 Representation of maximum TSD estimates based on the presence of volatile fatty acids (Vass et al., 1992).

correlate with the PMI. The 18 bodies were not embalmed and not autopsied; some were clothed, others unclothed, while others were placed in polyethylene bags in order to simulate different environments and all were placed on the ground in a wooded area. The time and cause of death were known and the environmental temperature was recorded during the decomposition period. Tissues from the brain, heart, lung, kidneys, liver, and muscle were sampled at regular intervals using a probe in order to reduce the degree of organ damage. Biomarker substances from the liver, kidneys, and heart proved the most useful in long-term estimation of the PMI, while the brain and liver were useful in the short term. The concentrations of gamma amino butyric acid (GABA), proline, methionine, and especially oxalic acid were found to be the most important biomolecules in determination of the PMI. It was found that ADDs were no longer sufficiently accurate to describe the PMIs and that a narrower time interval was required. They therefore used cumulative degree hours (CDHs) which were defined as the average temperature in °C for each 12-hour period cumulatively added. The two main features of the study were the appearance of glycolic acid in the PMI models and that every organ studied produced a varied assortment of complex biomarker information. A number of flow charts were produced which matched various concentrations of biomolecules with the PMI and two cases using biomarkers correlating with CDHs to estimate the PMI were cited.

Vass (2011) has continued to pursue research using a formula based on the time that VFAs cease to exude from a decomposing body, which he found to be 1285 ± 110 ADDs and at which soft tissue decomposition essentially ends. Stating that the four main factors influencing the rate of decomposition of a body were temperature, moisture, pH, and partial pressure of oxygen, Vass devised two new formulae to estimate the PMI, one for a body decomposing in aerobic conditions above ground and the other for a buried body decomposing in anaerobic conditions. The formulae incorporate an estimation of the amount of decomposition, the numerator; as well as the calculated effect of the environment on the decomposition, the denominator. The conditions for use of the first formula were that the body must be located above ground, in the preskeletonized phase and, if mummified, the tissue must be soft and pliable. The body must be at least 1 day after death, fairly intact, the temperature should be above 0°C, and the temperature and humidity should be corrected for the discovery site.

There should also be little or no adipocere tissue. The first formula is (Vass, 2011):

$$\text{PMI (aerobic)} = \frac{1285 \times (\text{Decomposition}/100)}{0.0103 \times \text{Temperature} \times \text{Humidity}} \qquad (5.1)$$

In this formula, the PMI is measured in days and *"decomposition"* is a percentage estimate of the extent of soft tissue decomposition, which should be determined by an experienced forensic investigator. "1285" is a constant representing the number of ADDs at which VFA liberation from soft tissue ceases and soft tissue decomposition effectively ends (Vass et al., 1992). "0.0103" is a constant, representing a line with a slope of 0.0103, an empirically determined measure based on the observation of the effect of moisture on human decomposition over a decade. "Temperature" is either the average temperature in °C on the day of discovery or the average temperature over a period of time at the site of discovery of the body, corrected after reference to the nearest national weather station data. "Humidity" is the average percentage humidity on the day of discovery or over a period of time, corrected after reference to the nearest national weather station data.

The conditions for use of the second formula were that the body should be undergoing anaerobic decomposition, usually buried; it must be in the preskeletonized phase and if mummified the tissue must be soft and pliable. It should not be in an area where the soil is highly saturated with water. The second formula is (Vass, 2011):

$$\text{PMI (anaerobic)} = \frac{1285 \times \left(\frac{\text{Decomposition}}{100}\right) \times 4.6 \times \text{Adipocere}}{0.0103 \times \text{Temperature} \times (\text{Soil moisture})} \qquad (5.2)$$

"1285" and "0.0103" are the same constants as used in the previous formula and "decomposition" is determined in the same way. "4.6" is a constant representing a slowdown in the rate of decomposition due to a lack of oxygen. Buried bodies have been estimated to take approximately eight times longer to decompose than bodies subjected to aerobic conditions. The value of 4.6 was determined from experiments by Vass over many years, in which surface-decomposing bodies were compared to buried bodies taking into account temperature and moisture parameters and allowing for the effects of the partial pressure of oxygen. "Adipocere" is an integer representing a percentage estimate of the amount of adipocere on the body and must be determined by a forensic investigator. The presence of adipocere slows decomposition by trapping moisture and decreasing the partial pressure of oxygen. Each 5% range is given an integer up to the value of 14 from a table devised after comparing adipocere formation in numerous surface and buried bodies and its effect on the rate of decomposition. It is this integer which is inserted in the formula. The "temperature" is that of the soil in the grave at the level of the body. It is measured by a thermocouple and compared with the surface temperature. The value inserted in the formula is determined by comparison with the temperature from the nearest weather station for the estimated time of burial adjusted accordingly. The "soil moisture" is a percentage determined by collecting a soil sample from beneath the body and comparing the weights before and after it is dried.

Vass (2011) claimed that the formulae worked well in the mid to eastern United States and he stated that he had applied them to many cases worldwide with success. However, the use of the formulae depended on the estimation of the stage of decomposition and amount of adipocere formation by an experienced observer, using percentage figures rather than a quantitative scale. The commonest source of error was when the time period exceeded 1285 days and it was also important that the body was in the preskeletonized stage. The estimation of the amount of adipocere was the weakest aspect of the second formula as not all bodies produced adipocere, and its estimation was difficult.

An important retrospective study, which stimulated others to research in a similar vein, was published in 2005 where, for the first time, decomposition was quantifiably staged and treated as a semicontinuous variable that correlated with temperature as measured by ADDs (Megyesi et al., 2005). Soft tissue decomposition was recognized as a sequential process with numerous small changes occurring throughout. These changes were quantified with numerical grading values to allow statistical testing of the relationship between decomposition, as the dependent variable and temperature as the independent variable. Sixty-eight cases of human remains were selected from forensic case files from throughout the United States. Fifty-seven corpses were found in the open in a variety of contexts and 11 were found indoors. Corpses which were burned, buried, submerged in water or with adipocere were excluded, as were children. However all corpses had a wide variety of clothing and 26 were naked or had very little clothing at all. All corpses showed evidence of insect access. The PMI was known in 20 cases from records and in 48 cases it was determined by insect evidence but it was less than a year in every case in order to select cases in which soft tissue was still present. The stage of decomposition was graded from photographs using a modification of the staging used by Galloway and colleagues (1989) (ie, fresh, early decomposition, advanced decomposition, and skeletonization). Within each stage there were descriptive subcategories which were given numerical values and because not all stages of decomposition applied equally to all parts of the body, it was divided into three parts for scoring purposes: the head and neck, the trunk, and the limbs. When the numerical values from the three parts were summated, the result amounted to a total body score (TBS). The lowest score possible was 4 and the highest 35. If the decomposition stage varied across one anatomical region, for example, an arm and a leg, the average of the two was taken. If the observed decomposition did not seem to match the sequence definitions, the numerical value assigned was one that matched the earlier stage of decomposition, because it was considered that the TBS should best reflect how much decomposition had taken place overall.

ADDs were calculated from the national weather service station data nearest to where each body was found and were defined as the product of the average daily temperature above $0°C$ (average of the maximum and minimum daily temperatures) from the time of death until discovery, with no correction carried out for distance or any other variable. As the temperature at which decomposition ceases is unknown, all temperatures that fell below $0°C$ were treated as $0°C$ because temperatures below 0 severely inhibit the chemical processes of decomposition and of bacterial growth. The quantitative analysis plotted TBS as the dependent variable against PMI and ADD as the independent variables. The relationships were not linear but, by log transforming both the ADD and PMI and squaring the TBS, an effective linear relationship was found, from which an equation could be produced. To find the PMI for any given case, the TBS would be calculated and this figure then substituted in the equation to calculate the figure for ADD. Once the ADD was known, the PMI could be calculated. Megyesi et al. (2005) stressed that the study only accounted for accumulated time and temperature as the main variables affecting decomposition and that other variables such as animal scavenging, sunlight, rainfall, and clothing might not be possible to quantify. Over 80% of the observed variation in human decomposition could be accounted for by the combination of elapsed time and temperature as reflected in ADDs.

The publication of this paper has stimulated researchers to use the concepts of ADDs and numerical grading systems of decomposition, in order to quantify the relationship between the rate of decomposition and temperature as the main variable.

Fitzgerald and Oxenham (2009) proposed another quantitative method of scoring decomposition when they devised a "degree of decomposition index" (DDI). The DDI used the general categories described by Galloway et al. (1989), but followed the method of Megyesi et al. (2005) which used the categories independently on separate body elements. It scored decomposition values from 0 to 5 by dividing the total scores of the stages observed on individual body elements by the number of body elements scored in order to make the DDI directly comparable to stages used in previous studies. Two pigs decomposing on the ground, one in semishade and one in full sun, were studied. Temperature and humidity data were recorded from each environment and data from the nearest Australian Bureau of Meteorology weather station were obtained. The DDI was compared with the four stages of decomposition of Rodriguez and Bass (1983) and the stages of Galloway et al. (1989). Fitzgerald and Oxenham did not use ADDs but instead used TSD measured in days as the independent variable. It was found that the carcass exposed to full sun became partly preserved by desiccation and adipocere formation, while the carcass in semishade disintegrated. The stages of decomposition described by Galloway et al. (1989) were found to be unusable as they were too narrow and too environmentally specific, while the broader categories described by Rodriguez and Bass (1983) were more useful for assigning a DDI for the carcasses. Despite the marked variation in the environments in which the two carcasses decomposed, the DDI curves of both were similar when compared with the TSD and smoother than the other methods of scoring decomposition. The results of regression modeling suggested that TSD correlated well with the DDI and accounted for 95% of the variation in decomposition between the carcasses while variations in the environment were not significant contributing factors.

However, Fitzgerald and Oxenham raised the important question as to whether or not TSD was purely a measure of transpired time or were other variables concealed within the measure such as environmental variables which were site-specific and specific to that particular TSD. The authors also found that there was no consistent relationship between the temperatures of the site and the temperatures recorded by the local weather station when calculations were being made for ADDs, a finding that did not bode well for the use of ADDs obtained retrospectively. It was also noted that although TSD and ADD both measured temperature and humidity over time, ADD had a distinct advantage over TSD in that TSD was reliant on location-specific seasonal data whereas ADD was not affected by seasonal temperature variation, only by location-specific patterns in the relationship between temperature and humidity. However, considering that TSD not only measured transpired time but also incorporated all environmental variables over the period of decomposition, whereas there was no consistent relationship between the measurement of ADDs at the decomposition site and at the local weather station, it was concluded that TSD was more appropriate for use in decomposition models than ADD.

A study by Adlam and Simmons (2007) monitored the decomposition of three groups of eight rabbit carcasses placed on soil on the ground, under cages to prevent scavenging, over a period of 3 weeks. One of each group of carcasses was disturbed at 3-day intervals while the other carcasses were only disturbed once for the purpose of taking observations. The aim of the study was to determine if repeated disturbance of carcasses affected the rate of decomposition. This study was of importance because in addition to taking environmental data measurements such as average temperature over 24-hour periods which was converted to ADDs, soil pH, weight, and temperatures of the carcasses, a visual qualitative decomposition scale was employed which was later converted to a numerical score. Adlam and Simmons showed that loss of weight was faster but the end weight was higher in the undisturbed samples although in the final analysis there was no difference in the time taken between the two groups to reach total skeletonization, that is, decomposition over time was not significantly altered by repeated physical disturbance. In both groups loss of weight correlated closely with increasing decomposition but weight loss and carcass temperature were significantly affected by repeatedly disturbing a carcass. The authors concluded that scoring decomposition directly yielded a more accurate assessment of the process and together with the use of ADDs might in future standardize measurements and allow comparisons with other studies.

Simmons and colleagues (2010) followed up this hypothesis by compiling data from a number of published and unpublished studies concerning decomposition and weight loss. The authors commented that in the past there had been an inability to directly compare results and observations from many studies because they varied in their methodology, geographical locale, climatic zone and season, species observed, and duration of observation. Yet other studies which had been based on retrospective forensic case work and data were not reported in a standardized form. It was suggested that the use of ADDs in documenting chronological time and temperature together in decomposition studies would allow comparison of studies across multiple and varied environments as ADDs represented the accumulation of thermal energy required for the chemical and biological reactions of decomposition to take place; when the same amount of thermal energy represented by ADDs was put into a carcass, the same amount of reaction, represented by the TBS, a measure of decomposition, would occur. Therefore, any animals exposed to fluctuating temperatures in any environment would show the same stage of decomposition for the same accumulation of degree days. They devised a formula to convert weight loss to a TBS, standardized after converting the different systems of scoring the TBS over many studies. Timescale data were converted to ADDs; not difficult in some controlled studies but in others an approximation had to be used because temperature data were not available for the duration of the studies. Data were collected from terrestrial, buried, and aquatic environments. Comparing log ADD with standardized TBS scores, Simmons and colleagues found a significant correlation over all studies. In all studies and contexts, at comparable ADDs, the presence of insects influenced the rate of decomposition by making it significantly faster. There was no significant difference in decomposition rate between indoor, buried, and submerged bodies, contexts in which insects had largely been excluded but more rapid decomposition occurred in bodies outdoors than bodies placed indoors, in surface compared with buried bodies, and in surface compared with submerged bodies. Variables such as penetrating trauma and percentage of body fat had no effect on the rate of decomposition. At comparable ADDs it is primarily the presence or absence of insects which has a significant effect on the rate at which a body will decompose, however Simmons and colleagues pointed to further research being required to refine the relationship between carcass size and the decomposition rate in the presence of insects. Simmons and colleagues concluded that although insects were the prime cause of rapidity of decomposition, in larger-sized carcasses, heat generated by larger maggot masses could increase the rate of decomposition. By comparison, in smaller carcasses the heat generated by smaller amounts of insects would be less but this might be offset by the smaller carcass decomposing more rapidly. Carcass size, however, had no influence on the rate of decomposition when insects were excluded. In contrast, a study carried out by Sutherland and colleagues (2013) in South Africa compared the decomposition rates between large pigs (60–90 kg) and small pigs (<35 kg). The result of this study, in which insects were not excluded, found that small pigs decomposed 2.82 times faster than the large pigs. Therefore body size did have an effect on the rate of decomposition.

Increasingly, studies are being published using ADDs as a proxy for the TSD (PMI) and modeling this parameter with graded decomposition scales in attempts to quantify the estimation of the PMI. Michaud and Moreau (2011) studied the relationship between decomposition stages and degree day accumulation by decomposing pig carcasses exposed over various seasons and over 3 years, in two large rural fields, 2.2 km apart. The purpose of the study was to verify the predictability of the decomposition stages used in forensic entomology and to build a degree day accumulation model applicable to various decomposition-related processes. They used a decomposition scale of five stages, fresh, bloated, active decay, advanced decay, and dry decay but because all stages were not of equal duration, a new scale was developed which allowed stages to be represented with realistic intervals instead of rigid values. ADD values were recorded by a data logger situated in one field and these were coordinated with a weather station situated in the other field. Statistical analysis was carried out in five stages: firstly, the calculation of ADDs since death; secondly, a scale was defined to represent decomposition with realistic intervals, called the degree day index; thirdly, a multiple regression analysis using ADDs and the decomposition scale was carried out to develop a decomposition index; fourthly, the probability that a carcass belonged to a given stage along the degree day index was calculated; and finally, the index was validated using data from a previous study. A multiple regression model was developed in which the onset of each decomposition stage, also known as the decomposition index, could be determined from the degree day index. The study supported the prediction that the physical condition of a carcass, as described by decomposition stages, was a reliable representation of the decomposition process and the model accounted for 97% of the variability in decomposition with respect to temperature. It also indicated that every stage of decomposition, except the active decay stage, had a high probability of occurring at a precise moment along the degree day index scale. When a degree day index had been developed for a given geographical area, the model required to be constructed from temperature records to calculate the ADDs. The ADD values could then be used to calculate decomposition indices for the same intervals. Michaud and Moreau admitted that some level of subjectivity existed in the discrimination between decomposition stages and they stressed the need for standard stage definitions that would reduce this possibility. However because the model incorporated adjustments for interyear, between season, and within season variations, it allowed for the development of prediction models throughout the year and in different geographical areas.

A longitudinal study of 10 human cadavers by Suckling (2011) tested the model of Megyesi et al. (2005) of scoring decomposition and its relationship to ADD. The effect of scavenging animals on the decomposition rate and its relationship to ADD was also factored into the study. The study found that scavenged bodies decomposed faster than protected cadavers and the Megyesi model, which had been developed from photographs, lacked precision in certain aspects. For example, Suckling found that in the central Texas environment, the external body could mummify but the deeper layers would still be undergoing soft tissue decomposition. Under the Megyesi system, mummification was given a higher numerical score than moist decomposition. However, Suckling observed the resumption of moist decomposition on two bodies which had been partly mummified, a situation not accounted for by Megyesi's method of scoring. Suckling also found a low success rate in using Megyesi's model to score bodies in the late stage of decomposition and she concluded that the model was not to be recommended in severely decomposed or skeletonized remains. Many variables were found to affect the TBS and future research was suggested to test for interobserver error in its estimation. This study by Suckling also did not support the assertion by Simmons et al. (2010) that data comparison from many different environments and temperatures regarding the stages of decomposition were comparable using TBS and ADD.

RESERVATIONS CONCERNING THE USE OF ADDs AND NUMERICAL BODY SCORING SYSTEMS

The concept of ADDs continues to be tested; a recent study was carried out on the high veldt of South Africa by Myburgh and colleagues (2013) in order to test the method in that specific environment. A total of 46 pigs with body weights varying between 38 and 91 kg were decomposed on a farm over a 232-day period. Thirty pigs were used to set up a standard to create a region-specific model and 16 pigs were used to validate the results. The state of decomposition was visually assessed three times a week until all tissues were desiccated, then once a week until skeletonized. The decomposition scoring method used was the one devised by Megyesi et al. (2005) and which resulted in a TBS. Maximum and minimum air temperatures were obtained, in order to calculate ADDs from a data logger on site and from a weather station 23 km from the site. The intraclass correlation coefficient between the two temperature recording sites was 0.9, indicating excellent agreement. Interobserver bias was tested by having an independent individual assessing the stages of decomposition and it was found to be negligible. Because ADD values were skewed on the original scale they were log transformed so as to be linearly related to TBS scores.

When TBS was plotted against ADD, the decomposition was exponential, being relatively linear in the early stages, regardless of the season (between 200 and 400 ADD) but becoming very variable with TBSs greater than 17. In these later stages of decomposition, the rate decreased to produce a plateau phase in which it remained stable and unchanged for long periods of time. Decomposition occurred faster in pigs deposited in summer compared with those deposited in winter after the TBS score became greater than 17. A predictive equation was developed to calculate the ADD for an unknown case. When TBS was regressed against log ADD an r^2 value of 0.623 was obtained, meaning that 62% of the variability in decomposition as reflected by the TBS was accounted for by ADD. In order to transform an ADD value into a PMI in an unknown case, an average of daily temperatures was recorded at a site or local weather station and added together from the day of discovery until the actual ADD equaled the estimated ADD. The PMI was then the number of days it took for these two values to become equal. However the results from the validation study on 16 pigs revealed that the PMI of only one pig fell within the lower limit of the 95% prediction interval. The PMIs of 11 pigs were underestimated while the PMIs of 4 pigs were overestimated, indicating that decomposition in that particular geographic area was too variable to allow accurate PMI estimations. The interobserver error in estimating the TBS, however, was excellent and was found to be repeatable 99.2% of the time.

In discussing the results, Myburgh and colleagues stated that although 62% of the variation found in the TBS scores could be explained with ADD, the 38% of the variability not accounted for by ADD, especially in the later stages, was possibly due to scavenging, seasonality, differences in humidity, and different rates of bacterial action. These factors could not be ignored and required further research to improve the accuracy of PMI determination but the authors commented that the TBS method was a good quantitative indicator of the stages of decomposition and the rate of change from one stage to another could be used to compare the rate of decomposition between specimens.

Studies in recent years have attempted to quantify the decomposition process as it affects the external appearance of a cadaver. Decomposition scores have been devised for pigs (Fitzgerald and Oxenham, 2009), rabbits (Adlam and Simmons, 2007), and humans (Megyesi et al., 2005), but comparison between species may diminish accuracy (Notter et al., 2009). As has been noted, increasing numbers of studies are designed to test Megyesi and colleagues' (2005) model of estimating the PMI. However, the method of estimating the TBS in this model may be too inaccurate because of the way it was derived. In the first instance the TBS was derived from 68 forensic cases investigated by different workers in a variety of geographical areas in 19 states of the United States. In addition the score was derived from perusing photographs of bodies, the majority of which were clothed so that only exposed parts of the body could be judged for the degree of decomposition. Only in a few bodies were the autopsy photographs used supplemented with detailed taphonomic data. Furthermore, the bodies were found in a number of different settings: indoors, outdoors, in shade, and in the sun, and finally the stages were subjectively modified into a sequential ranking so that the final decomposition scores reflected the total amount of accumulated decomposition that had occurred. In the previously quoted studies in which this model was used, the interpretation of this method of TBS may be too broad and too readily susceptible to individual interpretation. If a quantitative estimate of decomposition is to be of use in practice it must be simple to use and much more precise in its interpretation and description. The process of decomposition is not only a continuous, dynamic one but also a holistic one, affecting all body tissues and internal organs as well as the external appearance of the body. A further difficulty is that it is affected by many variable factors apart from temperature, such as humidity, environmental context, scavenging, insect activity, presence or absence of clothing, to name a few (Mann et al., 1990). If a body decomposition score can be devised that can take these factors into account and be easily employed then it may be useful forensically (Hayman, 2013).

Another problem with the use of the model proposed by Megyesi et al. (2005) concerns the accuracy of the compilation of ADDs, which in turn raises questions about the accuracy and precision of any model to estimate the PMI in which it is incorporated.

The principle of using temperature and time to measure plant development in heat units seems to have originated with Réaumur (1735). Réaumur totaled the mean daily temperatures for 91 days in Apr., May, and Jun. of that year in his locality and found the sum to be a nearly constant value for the development of any plant from year to year and he assumed that this constant value represented the amount of heat required for a plant to reach a given stage of maturity. Since that time and up to the present time horticulturists and entomologists have discussed the most accurate way of measuring temperature developmental units. Arnold (1959) discussed the difficulties in measurement of thermal heat units when they were used to define the development of certain crop varieties. These difficulties were the variation in temperatures between warm and cool parts of the same season, between warm and cool years, between northern and southern latitudes, and between low and high altitudes. These factors made determination of a threshold temperature difficult to calculate. Wang (1960) detailed several difficulties in the use of heat units to determine plant growth. These included the fact that plants responded differently to the same environmental factor during various stages of their life cycle and that the threshold temperature was considered a constant applied to the entire life cycle of a plant but this was unsound since the threshold values change with the advancing age of the plant. Wang also pointed out that heat units referred to the sum of the temperature, disguising the singularity of temperature changes and that growth was not linear with temperature change but followed a sigmoid curve. The heat unit system did not take into account many other factors which affected plant growth such as soil moisture, sunlight, solar radiation, wind and moisture, and duration of light and finally that the microclimatic problems regarding the representative quality of the temperature records used for heat unit evaluations were among the most complicated problems yet to be solved. Researchers continued to search for a more accurate method to account for growth as expressed by heat units. Allen (1976) published a modified sine wave method for calculating degree days but this was found to differ in different geographical areas and required a method of correction for local bias using linear regression. Pruess (1983) discussed the various methods to that date of measuring degree days for the estimation of insect development and he suggested ways in which they could be improved. He commented that one reason all insect development models had not found practical application was that they provided no more accuracy than the use of calendar dates and that if degree day measurements were to be used in practice some compromise might be necessary between precision and utility. It would also be desirable if similar models could be used for both insects and plants.

Vass and colleagues (1992) appear to have been the first researchers to introduce the concept of ADDs into the study of human decomposition and they quote the definition of ADDs given by Edwards et al. (1987). The 1987 paper discusses temperature development units for insects which could also be used to determine plant development. The use of these units is based on the knowledge that insects as well as plants are poikilothermic, that is, unlike mammals which incorporate their own body temperature regulatory mechanism, insect and plant development depends on ambient temperature. Each species has a threshold temperature below which development ceases and a maximum temperature above which development slows or stops. Eventually the right amount of temperature is accumulated for development to be complete. Edwards, Chaney, and Bergman present three methods to compute developmental temperature units. The first method, degree days, is defined as the amount of biological activity caused by one degree above the threshold for one day. They do not, however, define the "threshold." Vass et al. (1992) define ADDs as being determined by taking the sum of the average daily temperatures, in degrees Centigrade, for however long a corpse has been decomposing and Megyesi et al. (2005) calculate ADDs for each case by adding together all average daily temperatures from death until discovery, using $0°C$ as the base temperature because freezing temperatures severely inhibit biological processes such as bacterial growth. In a similar way to the development of insects and plants, decomposing cadavers are poikilo-thermic with the chemical reactions driving the decomposition process dependent on environmental temperature; some reactions will slow down with falling temperatures and speed up with rising temperatures but the threshold and range of temperatures will vary depending on the reaction. The temperature threshold at which human decomposition ceases is not known. Vass et al. (1992) state that decomposition still occurs when the temperature falls to $0°C$ because of the increased salt concentrations in the human body, Micozzi (1991) states that no putre-faction occurs at a temperature less than $4°C$ and Janaway et al. (2009) state that decomposition is prevented below $-5°C$ as both enzymatic and microbial action will be halted. However, none of these authors present any research to substantiate these statements. Putrefactive gas was progressively found to form over a 3-day period in the heart and liver of a cadaver stored in a mortuary refrigerator at $4°C$ (Singh et al., 2009). In the process of human decomposition there are very many chemical reactions occurring simultaneously and not all will depend upon the same maximum and minimum temperature thresholds. The environmental temperature in which any specific body decomposes will also vary depending on many other factors (Mann et al., 1990). At the present time, therefore, it is not possible to define single threshold tem-peratures below or above which human decomposition ceases, which means that the definition of ADDs is still open to interpretation, as is its use in any study.

Recent research has also raised the question of the accuracy of temperature data collection in human decomposition studies because the geographical separation between the death scene and the nearest weather station necessitates ambient temperature correction. A note of caution about using local weather station data when compiling ADDs to provide minimum PMI estimates when blowfly larval growth is used to estimate the TSD was reported by Archer (2004) in Australia. Archer commented that obtaining temperature data from a body discovery site was essential in order to calculate minimum PMI estimates. One common practice was to collect temperature data from a body discovery site for comparison with temperature data from a local weather station. A regression equation was constructed to compare temperatures at the body discovery site with those measured simultaneously at the local weather station. The equation was then used to retrospectively correct ambient temperatures measured at the weather station during the period the body was thought to have lain in situ. Other workers simply made a note of differences between the site temperature data and the weather station data, taking the differences into account when performing a minimum PMI; however, how this was done remained unclear. There were no data available on whether regression relationships between body discovery sites and weather stations were likely to vary over time, and no data examining the accuracy of correlation relationships between the sites and the weather stations. Correlation data should ideally be collected immediately following body removal and when weather patterns and temperatures were similar to the period the body lay in situ, but this might not be possible because of logistical problems and changing weather patterns between the time of body discovery and the collection of correlation data.

Archer compared temperature data from six hypothetical body discovery test sites, recorded with data loggers, with temperature data from one local weather station for the same period. All hypothetical sites were within a 5-km radius from the weather station and the study was designed to test whether the timing of the correlation period after body removal affected the accuracy of retrospective weather data correction. Five data logging periods were employed, the first period called the "body in situ period" recorded temperatures for 7 consecutive days that a hypothetical body would have actually lain at the site. Four other correlation periods of 10 days consecutive temperature recordings, with increasing intervals between, were carried out. Statistical analysis of the data obtained was then carried out. Archer found that weather data retrospectively corrected using a correlation method, provided a more accurate representation of site temperatures than uncorrected data and a more accurate calculation of thermal units if ADDs were used. However the degree of improvement was highly variable between correlation periods and did not always improve the accuracy of weather data. This finding emphasized the need to use generous margins when predicting an estimate of minimum PMI. A further finding was that weather conditions during the correlation and "body in situ" periods affected the outcome of the retrospective correction, in that the mean estimated site temperatures for the "body in situ" period rose significantly with time after the event, thought to be because average temperatures rose throughout the experiment as spring progressed to summer.

Archer concluded that further research was required to determine the effects of season, distance from the weather station, sun and shade, and indoor and outdoor settings, all of which could impact on the accuracy of the technique. Increase in the time after body removal before correlation data were collected could decrease the benefits gained by retrospective correction and this decrease was due to differences between weather conditions during the correlation and "body in situ" periods.

Johnson et al. (2012) published further research examining additional factors affecting ambient temperature corrections of weather station data in forensic entomology. Ambient temperature data were collected from 16 hypothetical body discovery sites in two different states, in two different seasons, and across a number of geographical regions. They were then compared with temperature data from the nearest weather station which were all within 15 km of the body discovery sites. The accuracy of retrospective weather data collection was tested by four experiments: firstly, to test the length of the correlation period; secondly, to test the distance between body discovery sites and weather stations; thirdly, to test the periodicity of ambient temperature measurements; and finally, to assess correlation accuracy in casework scenarios.

The authors' results showed that correlation gave significant improvement over raw weather data regardless of the length of the correlation period, improving the accuracy of body site discovery temperature estimation by more than $1(\pm 0.5)°C$ in 96% of correlations. Secondly, there was no effect of distance on the accuracy of correlations for either experimental season. Thirdly, results suggested that 30-minute and 3-hourly temperature measurement intervals provided improvement over raw weather data but twice-daily measurements did not.

Lastly, when assessing correlation accuracy in casework scenarios, the greater the difference between the average weather station temperatures for the in situ body period and the average weather station temperatures for the correlation period, the greater was the accuracy. In those cases where the accuracy was not good, it was made acceptable by extending the duration of the correlation period. Johnson, Wallman, and Archer concluded that retrospective ambient temperature correction of weather station temperature was a robust technique, the accuracy of which was not affected by season, the length of the correlation period, or distances up to 15 km between the site of body discovery and the weather station. The accuracy, however, was diminished if there was >5°C difference between weather station, body in situ, and correlation data. Extending the length of the correlation period from 2 to 5 days could overcome this error and in fact the authors recommended the collection of correlation data for 10 days when possible, and at intervals not longer than every 30 minutes or 3 hours.

A third study in Arizona by Dabbs (2010) addressed the question of the validity of using temperature data from the National Weather Service for calculating the PMI, by examining the correlation between temperature data collected at a study site with temperature data from the two closest weather stations, 5.7 and 9.9 km distant. Data loggers, which had been tested prior to commencement of the study and found to be very accurate, were placed at the study site to collect temperature data for 154 days which were then converted to a daily average temperature by averaging the highest and lowest hourly temperature over a 24-hour period. Daily average temperatures were collected from the two weather stations closest to the study site, at distances of 5.7 and 9.9 km, for the same period of 154 days. Dabbs used the ADD data obtained from the three sites, incorporating it in the model published by Megyesi et al. (2005) to calculate theoretical PMIs for the three sites of data collection. PMI was calculated in days for each of the three sites for TBSs ranging from 3 to 27.

The results revealed significant differences between the study site and the weather station sites. There was an average daily temperature 0.6°C (SD 1.1°C) higher at the weather station farthest away (9.9 km) from the study site than at the study site and the largest daily difference was 5.5°C. The difference in average daily temperature between the study site and the nearest weather station (5.7 km) was 2.0°C (SD 0.97°C) higher on average at the weather station with a maximum difference of 6.5°C on 1 day. When the PMI was calculated for TBS scores between 3 and 27, the average difference between the study site and the closest weather station was 5.8 days while the average difference between the study site and the farthest away weather station was 3.55 days. Dabbs concluded that blind utilization of temperature data from the nearest weather station to a body discovery site was not appropriate for the estimation of the PMI using ADDs and that further research was required to develop a protocol to test the accuracy of use of weather station data to estimate the PMI before such data could be used in forensic cases.

In recent times researchers have been increasingly using a quantitative body decomposition score together with ADDs in modeling the TSD in humans (Galloway et al., 1989; Vass et al., 1992; Megyesi et al., 2005; Fitzgerald and Oxenham, 2009). However the methods of compiling and scoring vary considerably. If studies are to be comparable a standard method of quantitatively scoring the decomposing human body is required. One such method has recently been proposed based on the examination of standardized autopsy reports (Hayman and Oxenham, 2016; Hayman, 2013). In Australia there is a national database, the National Coronial Information System (NCIS), which has listed all cases reported to a coroner since the year 2000. This provides a valuable source of information concerning all decomposed human bodies reported since that time. All autopsy reports are listed in a standard form giving detailed descriptions of the decomposition affecting the various organs of the body as well as the external appearance of the body. Police reports concerning details of the discovery and, in some cases, an estimation of the time of death of the deceased, are also recorded. From these reports it was possible to compile quantitative decomposition scores for certain key organs: brain, heart, liver, and spleen as well as external appearance of the body, which appeared to decompose in a regular manner with the passage of time up to 14 days. An unexpected finding from the NCIS database was that the great majority of decomposed bodies found in Australian conditions are found indoors in houses or units and so the models relate to this environment. Each of the organ scores when totaled gave a TBS. A total dataset of 239 cases in which the TSD was known within 1 day was compiled from the states of New South Wales, Victoria,

Tasmania, and the Northern Territory. Datasets were also compiled for each of these states separately.

Bivariate regression modeling was carried out with TSD as the dependent variable and the TBS as the independent variable. Good correlation was found between TSD and TBS for all datasets. In the total dataset (239 cases) the correlation coefficient r was 0.874 and r^2 was 0.764, indicating that 76.4% of the variability in the determination of the TSD was accounted for by the TBS. The standard error of the estimate (SEE) was 2.009. However, 23.6% of the variability was accounted for by some other unknown factor or factors. Results for the datasets of each state were even better, for example, New South Wales, $r = 0.970$, $r^2 = 0.941$ (SEE = 0.755); Victoria, $r = 0.976$, $r^2 = 0.953$ (SEE = 0.733). As temperature is the other major variable affecting decomposition, various combinations of temperature data compiled from weather stations nearest to where each body was found, such as average daily temperature, average daily high and low temperatures, and final day temperatures as well as humidity parameters, were factored in to multiple regression models using TSD as the dependent variable but no parameter gave a statistically significant result. Although ADDs were compiled, this measure could not be used in a statistical model as it correlates directly with the TSD, that is, it is another measure of the passage of time.

Models were compiled for each state and territory which gave an estimate of the TSD but only up to 14 days; after this time the assessment of the TBS became increasingly difficult and inaccurate. Temperature was arguably an important variable and although this could not be shown in a regression model, its importance was illustrated when fitted and observed relationships were compiled for each of the states and the Northern Territory. These clearly showed that in the Northern Territory, a tropical region with a much higher average temperature year round, a body decomposed at a faster rate than any of the southern states over the same period of time.

This study showed the importance of compiling accurate data concerning not only decomposed bodies but all forensic cases generally on a national basis. Australia is almost alone in the world in the compilation of such data but in many countries the collection of such data may prove impossible because of organizational and political reasons.

CONCLUSION

The present trend is to use ADDs in conjunction with TBS in order to find more accurate models to quantify the PMI; however, at the present time the determination of ADDs is inaccurate because the temperature at which decomposition ceases is not known and the actual temperature during which time a body is decomposing is also difficult to measure. The decomposition process is caused by many chemical reactions, many of which may have different temperature thresholds controlling their progression. In addition the ambient temperature will also vary depending on the environment in which the body decomposes and other factors such as maggot activity, animal scavenging, and wounds to a body which affect the rate of decomposition. The use of a TBS suffers from the inaccuracy of there being no standard method of descriptively defining one or uniformly quantifying one so that different studies can be standardized and compared. It may be that further improved accuracy in estimating the TSD must await the advent and development of quantum computing which may be able in future to factor in the multiple variables involved in the process of decomposition.

REFERENCES

Adlam, R.E., Simmons, T., 2007. The effect of repeated physical disturbance on soft tissue decomposition – are taphonomic studies an accurate reflection of decomposition? J. Forensic Sci. 52 (5), 1007–1014.

Allen, J.C., 1976. A modified sine wave method for calculating degree days. Environ. Entomol. 5, 388–396.

Archer, M.S., 2004. The effect of time after body discovery on the accuracy of retrospective weather station ambient temperature corrections in forensic entomology. J. Forensic Sci. 49 (3), 1–7.

Arnold, C.Y., 1959. The determination and significance of the base temperature in a linear heat system. Proc. Am. Soc. Hortic. Sci. 74, 430–445.

Dabbs, G.R., 2010. Caution! All data are not created equal: the hazards of using National Weather Service data for calculating accumulated degree days. Forensic Sci. Int. 202, e49–e52.

Edwards, R., Chaney, B., Bergman, M., 1987. Temperature developmental units for insects. Pest Crop Newslett. Purdue Univ. 2, 5–6.

Fitzgerald, C.M., Oxenham, M., 2009. Modelling time-since-death in Australian temperate conditions. Aust. J. Forensic Sci. 41 (1), 27–41.

Fuller, M.E., 1934. Insect inhabitants of carrion: a study in animal ecology. Aust. Counc. Sci. Ind. Res. Bull. 82, 1–62.

Galloway, A., et al., 1989. Decay rates of human remains in an arid environment. J. Forensic Sci. 34 (3), 607–616.

Hayman, J., 2013. Towards a More Accurate Estimation of the Time Since Death in Human Bodies Found Decomposed in Australian Conditions. Ph.D. Thesis. Australian National University, Canberra.

Hayman J., Oxenham M., 2016. Estimation of the time since death in decomposed bodies found in Australian conditions. Aust. J. Forensic Sci. 48 (2), 171–185.

Henssge, C., Madea, B., 2007. Estimation of the time since death. Forensic Sci. Int. 165, 182–184.

Howden, A.T., 1950. The Succession of Beetles on Carrion. Unpublished Thesis. North Carolina State College, Raleigh, NC.

Janaway, R.C., Percival, S.L., Wilson, A.S., 2009. Decomposition of human remains. In: Percival, S.L. (Ed.), Microbiology and Aging. Springer Science and Business Media, LLC.

Johnson, A.P., Wallman, J.F., Archer, M.S., 2012. Experimental and casework validation of ambient temperature corrections in forensic entomology. J. Forensic Sci. 57 (1), 215–221.

Mann, R.W., Bass, W.M., Meadows, L., 1990. Time since death and decomposition of the human body: variables and observations in case and experimental field studies. J. Forensic Sci. 35 (1), 103–111.

Mégnin P., 1894. La Faune des Cadavres. Application d'Entomologie à la Médecine Légale. Gauthier et fils, Paris.

Megyesi, M.S., Nawrocki, S.P., Haskell, N.H., 2005. Using accumulated degree days to estimate the post-mortem interval from decomposed human remains. J. Forensic Sci. 50 (3), 1–9.

Michaud, J.-P., Moreau, G., 2011. A statistical approach based on accumulated degree-days to predict decomposition-related processes in forensic studies. J. Forensic Sci. 56 (1), 229–232.

Micozzi, M.S., 1991. Post-mortem Change in Human and Animal Remains: A Systematic Approach. Charles C. Thomas, Springfield, IL, p. 40. Ch. 5.

Myburgh, J., et al., 2013. Estimating the post-mortem interval (PMI) using accumulated degree days (ADD) in a temperate region of South Africa. Forensic Sci. Int. 229, 165.e1–165.e6.

Notter, S.J., Stuart, B.H., Rowe, R., Langlois, N., 2009. The initial changes of fat deposits during the decomposition of human and pig remains. J. Forensic Sci. 54 (1), 195–201.

Payne, J.A., 1965. A summer carrion study of the baby pig *Sus scrofa* Linnaeus. Ecology 46 (5), 592–602.

Pruess, K.P., 1983. Day-degree methods for pest management. Environ. Entomol. 12 (3), 613–619.

Réaumur, R.A.F., 1735. Observations du thérmomètre faites à Paris pendant l'année 1735, comparées avec celles qui ont été faites sous la ligne; à l'Isle de France, à Alger et en quelques-unes de nos Isles de l'Amérique. Mémoires de l'Académie des Sciences 545–576.

Reed, H.B., 1958. A study of dog carcass communities in Tennessee with special reference to the insects. Am. Midl. Nat. 59 (1), 213–245.

Rodriguez, W.C., Bass, W.M., 1983. Insect activity and its relationship to decay rates of human cadavers in east Tennessee. J. Forensic Sci. 28 (2), 423–432.

Simmons, T., Adlam, R.E., Moffatt, C., 2010. Debugging decomposition data – comparative taphonomic studies and the influence of insects and carcass size and decomposition rate. J. Forensic Sci. 55 (1), 8–13.

Singh, M.K.C., O'Donnell, C., Woodford, N.M., 2009. Progressive gas formation in a deceased person during mortuary storage demonstrated on computed tomography. Forensic Sci Med. Pathol. 5, 236–242.

Suckling, J.K., 2011. A Longitudinal Study on the Outdoor Human Decomposition Sequence in Central Texas. MSc Thesis. Texas State University.

Sung Tz'u, 1186–1249. The Washing Away of Wrongs. Translated from the Chinese by McKnight, B.E., 1981. University of Michigan, Ann Arbor, p. 87.

Sutherland, A., Myburgh, J., Steyn, M., Becker, P.J., 2013. The effect of body size on the rate of decomposition in a temperate region of South Africa. Forensic Sci. Int. 231, 257–262.

Vass, A.A., et al., 1992. Time since death determinations in human cadavers using soil solution. J. Forensic Sci. 37 (5), 1236–1253.

Vass, A.A., et al., 2002. Decomposition chemistry of human remains: a new methodology for determining the post-mortem interval. J. Forensic Sci. 47 (3), 542–553.

Vass, A.A., 2011. The elusive post-mortem interval. Forensic Sci. Int. 204, 34–40.

Wang, J.Y., 1960. A critique of the heat unit approach to plant response studies. Ecology 41 (4), 785–790.

Printed in Great Britain
by Amazon